LIFT YOUR PASTOR

Becoming A Pastor's Advocate

By
Dr. Michael Lewis
and Andy Spencer

"Michael has such a heart for Pastors, his and Andy's experience along with passionate concern for others makes their writing a great read with much needed helps."

JOHNNY HUNT, PASTOR
FIRST BAPTIST CHURCH WOODSTOCK

"Lift Your Pastor is more than just a book by great authors. This is a timely book filled with practical and spiritual truths from two Godly men who are willing to "do the book" in their friendship with each other and in their own lives. The story of how God has used these men in the ministry through advocating, not only encourages me, but it will encourage you! If you are a pastor and feel alone in the ministry "Lift Your Pastor" is must have."

TOMMY ESTES, PASTOR
FAITH MISSIONARY BAPTIST CHURCH
ROUND ROCK, TEXAS

"Who teaches the teacher? Who coaches the coach? Who pastors the Pastor? Michael and Andy have found the solution to the pastor issue. They have written the playbook for how to support the pastors. It's a win-win for you as a Pastor and you as an accountability partner. Everyone is on the same page and yet personalizing your own play book. Solid, biblical truth put together to keep you actively on the Kingdom team. It's all here and ready to be played out. Get two and share the Word."

BILL BEBEE
10:27 MINISTRIES

"With so much pastoral discouragement today what a blessing to have this excellent resource. Pastor Michael Lewis and Andy Spencer have given the church a wonderful gift. Their book Lift Your Pastor will infuse hope and joy back into a weary pastor through the influence and encouragement of an advocate. My desire is that every layperson make sure that his or her pastor has a copy of Lift Your Pastor. If you are a pastor, then please read and be blessed."

DANNY FORSHEE, PASTOR
GREAT HILLS BAPTIST CHURCH
AUSTIN, TX

"The life of a pastor is filled with many life moments: some breathtaking and others, well, not so much so. This is why "all" pastors need an advocate, someone who will stand beside you at all times. Andy Spencer lives out what he writes. He absolutely loves pastors and has dedicated his life's work to help pastors reach their full potential. I whole heartedly endorse and recommend that you pour through these pages of encouragement and witness."

DR. RICH CARNEY, EXECUTIVE DIRECTOR
ABBA (AUSTIN BRIDGE BUILDERS ASSOCIATION)

Title: LIFT Your Pastor…Becoming A Pastor's Advocate

Author: Dr. Michael Lewis and Andy Spencer

Unless otherwise indicated, all Scripture quotations are taken from Christian Standard Version of the Bible. (2009); Nashville: Holman Bible Publishers.

Published by: Engedi Publishing LLC, in the United States of America

DEDICATIONS

I dedicate this writing to the glory of the Great Shepherd of the sheep who gives His shepherds of local churches lifting friendships through all seasons of ministry. I am grateful for the faithful and loving marriage relationship with Liliana, my wife of 26 years, and the encouraging love of our daughters - Charity, Faith and Hope. It is a joy to partner together with the 'best-est buddy on the planet,' Andy Spencer, to write a chronicle of our sustaining friendship, a true Biblical example of a Jonathan-David relationship. May every pastor be inspired that there are friends and advocates like Andy!

— Dr. Michael Lewis, Senior Pastor, Roswell Street Baptist Church

I would like to thank all the pastors that have had an impact on my life. From my youth pastor at St John's Methodist in Corpus Christ (Jim Farris) to my current pastor and friend at Great Hills Baptist Church (Danny Forshee). College Pastors, Young Married Pastors, Children's Pastors and a wide variety of Christian leaders in my life. I have been very blessed in my life by the Pastors who have taught and lead me in my Christian walk. I would also like to thank my wife Kathy for steadfastness in standing by me though these times. My daughters Deanna and Andrea are a constant source of blessings. Finally I would like to thank my best friend on the planet, Michael Lewis. Writing this book together has emphasized what an important and faithful friendship we have. My prayer is that this book would lead Pastors to have a close personal friendship in their lives and train up those who would fill that role of a "pastor's advocate."

— Andy Spencer

SPECIAL THANKS

Camille Minor – Editor
Suzanne Sarto (CricketGrafix) – Graphic Design
Terri Snead – Great Commandment Network

TABLE OF CONTENTS

TABLE OF CONTENTS

PREFACE

Ecclesiastes 4:9-12

"Two are better than one because they have a good reward for their efforts. For if either falls, his companion can LIFT him up; but pity the one who falls without another to LIFT him up. Also, if two lie down together, they can keep warm; but how can one person alone keep warm? And if someone overpowers one person, two can resist him. A cord of three strands is not easily broken."

Why We (Andy and Michael) Wrote this Book

One of the loneliest place on the earth can be serving as a pastor of a local church. Many pastors would agree with that statement. I (Michael) know in my heart that, having had the privilege of serving as a pastor for over 27 years, I have faced many times of loneliness in the ministry. The Lord has certainly been faithful to meet my needs and comfort me in times of aloneness, but it's been "an advocate" who has been the hands, feet and arms of Jesus when I needed it the most. Webster's Dictionary tells us that an advocate is someone who promotes and supports the interests of another. I have discovered that I needed an advocate in my life and ministry. For me, it's been my friend, Andy Spencer who has supported me and lifted up the needs of my family. God graciously involved Andy to remove my aloneness!

> *...an advocate is someone who promotes and supports the interests of another.*

Loneliness in ministry leads to discouragement, disillusionment and even the possibility of leaving the ministry all together. For a pastor, discouragement can easily come if no one ever indicates that he measures up or affirms his calling. In a September, 2015 the Pastor Protection Research Study, surveyed 1500 American pastors (LifeWay Research (lifewayresearch.com) conducted the research in partnership with North American Mission Board of the Southern Baptist Convention), and discovered that:

- 54% of the surveyed 1500 pastors agreed the role of pastor is frequently overwhelming.
- Over 8 out of 10 pastors agreed they feel they must be on call 24 hours a day.
- 48% of pastors agreed they often feel the demands of ministry are greater than they can handle.
- 15% of pastors felt they do not have a day of rest at least once a week.
- 1 out of every 3 pastors agreed they feel isolated as a pastor.
- Only 29% of churches have a plan for the pastor to periodically have a sabbatical leave.
- 5 out of 10 pastors agreed they are often concerned about the financial security of their family.
- More than 1 in 3 pastors agreed ministry demands keep them from spending time with their family.
- More than 1 in 5 pastors agreed that their family resents the demands of pastoral ministry.

The Pastor Protection research highlights the reasons why many full-time pastors often become discouraged and lose their passion for carrying out the ministry in their local church. Disillusionment can cause pastors to grow weary and feel deeply alone in ministry. For instance, when a sermon series does not produce the desired results, or when an evangelistic outreach does not go as planned, it can leave the pastor feeling vulnerable and ineffective, and thus produce questions about ministry vision or even ministry calling. There is an alarming rate of dropout among pastors in North America because many who get discouraged and disillusioned struggle to withstand the inevitable pressures that come with life and ministry. In his letter to Timothy, the Apostle Paul described this phenomenon as a condition wherein people have made a shipwreck of their faith. That's why today's ministry leaders need an advocate – someone who can come alongside and help buoy their faith in Jesus as well as their passion for ministry.

Disillusionment can cause pastors to grow weary and feel deeply alone in ministry.

This book is written with the hope of removing the aloneness that is often associated with a pastoral ministry. We also hope to reveal how pastors can open their heart to experience friendship with a "pastor's advocate". This advocate will be able to offer encouragement and support to the pastor personally and then champion the pastor's vision in the work of ministry. Finally, this resource seeks to encourage church leaders to become the kind of advocate who can help the pastor – not only to survive in ministry, but to thrive in it!

INTRODUCTION

Michael Lewis' Story

I (Michael) am simply and sincerely a pastor. I've served as a pastor for over twenty seven years in local churches throughout South Carolina, Georgia, Texas, and Florida. I surrendered to the call of ministry at 17 years of age. When I was 21- years-old, God called me to my first pastoral work.

My first church was a small, rural church in upstate South Carolina. I started ministry with plenty of challenge. The church was in a condition of decline and had even considered closing its doors. Thankfully, the Lord blessed this first ministry calling and increased the congregation from 50 people to over 200; it was an all-embracing ministry experience that impacted various cultures within the community. After South Carolina, I was called to pastor a second church. It also came with a unique challenge, for God called me to serve my home church in Richmond Hill, Georgia. While it wasn't always easy leading the church where I had grown up, God favored and encouraged the church in evangelism and outreach; we were able to experience significant spiritual and numerical growth In our third ministry calling, I followed a pastor who had served the church for 34 years. It was challenging at times to be the new pastor among such long-standing traditions, but the Lord allowed me to successfully help the church transition from a state of plateau to vibrant growth. My fourth pastorate was at a 139-year-old church in Plant City, Florida. The Lord blessed the church with a powerful Gospel-awakening which positively impacted the surrounding community. So as you can see, I've had a wide-variety of pastoral experiences. Each ministry setting has had it's blessings and it's challenges.

After these many years of serving as a local church pastor, God called me to a new season of ministry as the Executive Director of Pastoral Care and Development at the North American Mission Board - SBC. My role was to support and care for the pastors and families of over 46,000 Southern Baptist churches throughout North America. During this time the Lord graciously allowed me to encourage 15,000 pastors through marriage retreats, pastor round-tables, conferences, resources and retreats. Prior to my calling to NAMB, there was no strategic care for SBC pastors; but now by God's wisdom, they now have a continuum of care for them through the Pastoral Care Line with Focus on the Family and many kingdom resources developed through strategic partnerships.

And now, God has stirred my heart and called our family to pastor the local church again. I currently serve as lead pastor at Roswell Street Baptist Church in Marietta, Georgia. Roswell Street is in prayerful hopes of revitalization and community impact with the Gospel.

Throughout my journey as a pastor, I'm extremely grateful that God provided a godly wife to accompany me. I'm married to Liliana, who is from Mexico City, Mexico and we have three daughters; Charity, Faith and Hope. By God's amazing grace, the Lord has allowed our family to experience joy and victory through all the challenges of the pastorate. As we walk through this book together, I'll describe some of the ups and downs of our ministry experience, so that advocates will better understand the challenges that pastor often face.

Andy's Story

My name is Andy Spencer and I currently live in Austin, Texas. I was raised in a businessman's home. I would describe my father as the ultimate southern gentleman. From an early age, I was taught all aspects of business; my dad taught me how to take care of customers, sell a product, take care of employees, and build a successful business.

I was saved by the grace of God through a personal faith in Christ at the age of 13. The pastor gave a message about Jesus' saving grace during youth camp in Kerrville, Texas. He told us that we were all sinners and were far from God. He reminded us that all we had to do was believe in our hearts and confess Jesus with our mouths and that would begin our relationship with God. It was at that moment that I discovered my need for a Savior, and began my own personal relationship with Jesus Christ.

As a young teenager, I was constantly worried about what success actually looked like. Sometimes I would ask myself, "Will I be successful in life?" While I was growing up, we experienced the inevitable ups and downs of a family business. There were times when I wasn't sure what these uncertain financial times would have on my generation, but after having an encounter with Jesus , many of these concerns and worries went away and I began to trust Him more with my future. In college, I was able to learn more about the world of business and had the opportunity to learn what it means to be a leader.

A leader is someone who lives so that others will follow; a leader is a person who lives a life worthy of being followed. After I finished my college education, I found myself in several churches where I began to understand how difficult it is to be a pastor. I found out that a pastor's job is much more than the Sunday morning services. A pastor's job is 24 hours a day, 7 days a week. I learned the simple truth that being a pastor is hard. For instance, there are people who want to influence a pastor from very different points of view. There are people who want to support the pastor and people who are not interested in providing support at all. These observations led me to conclude that a pastor needs a friend. A pastor needs an advocate.

A leader is a person that lives a life worthy of being followed.

For the purpose of this book, we're going to use the term, "Pastor's Advocate". How did we get this term? We've already talked about the definition of advocate: someone who supports and promotes the interest of another. I began using the word, "advocate" in my career as a salesperson. At one time in our company, we were perplexed about what label to add to our business cards. My role in the company was a salesperson, but we realized that so many people thought of the polyester-suit-wearing-used-car-salesman when they heard the word, "salesperson." We concluded there had to be a better name for this position.

About this time, leaders in the industry started to use the word, "advocate". We could become customer-advocates. We could be someone who truly promotes and supports the interest of another. We quickly realized that the universal truth in the business world, "Buy low, sell high," does have a tendency to get in the way of advocacy. Some of our biggest business successes came when we had a relationship with a mutual goal. One of my customers said it like this, "Andy, the reason I like meeting with you and doing business with your company is that, after our conversations, I feel like both our businesses will succeed because of this relationship." I learned that this is the outcome we want in all of our relationships.

I have been supported and served by several great pastors who were wholeheartedly involved in my life. Beginning with the pastor who preached the Gospel when I was 13-years-old, I've seen God weave pastors into my life in meaningful ways. My youth pastor taught me to be a leader both inside the church, as well as reach people outside the church. Several other pastors have reminded me that pastors are just real people who have families and real needs like anyone else. Pastors do have a divine calling on their lives, but they also have an earthly need for friends. Not everyone realizes that pastors are human beings too.

In the second half of my life (using Bob Buford's phrase from the book, Halftime), I have now made it my mission and goal to help pastors and their families. My heart's desire is to provide support to as many pastors as God will allow me. The strategy I use is a leadership development model using peer-to-peer interaction as a learning tool since pastors often learn best from one another. Over the years, I discovered that the peer-to-peer, gifted learning retreats have been an effective tool for pastors to be both encouragers and challengers for one another. Another prayerful ambition is encouraging and equipping leaders of the church to be encouragers for their pastors. To be a pastor's advocate means: no hidden or selfish agenda, no ambition of your own, but simply a pure commitment to be a friend and an encourager for the pastor and family.

...no hidden or selfish agenda, no ambition of your own, but simply a pure commitment to be a friend and an encourager for the pastor and family.

Just like Michael, I have an amazing, godly wife who has been my partner through all of life's adventures. I've been married to Kathy for 27 years now. We live in Austin, Texas and have two daughters, Deanna and Andrea. These wonderful girls are in their late teens; and all three ladies are the loves of my life. I love my family; and out of a healthy relationship with my family, we join together to love and bless pastors and their families.

More Words from Michael

I (Michael) had the joy of serving Andy, Kathy, Deanna, and Andrea as their pastor in Austin, Texas. In those years, Andy stood with me as an advocate for my family and ministry. From our first conversation, Andy and I discovered that we had many mutual interests. We were in the same season of life with our families and careers. Andy, as a business leader, was leading his business to grow with excellence, and as a young pastor I had been called to lead the church into excellence, as we carried the Gospel to the surrounding community.

Andy has been an advocate for me simply because he's been a faithful friend. Proverbs 17:17 states this, "A friend loves at all times, and a brother is born for a difficult time." Andy loved me, his chosen friend, when I was popular and everyone wanted to be around me as a pastor; and he has loved me when I was unpopular and many did not like me. Andy has always been someone who would speak words of life and encouragement into my heart. And during my downtimes, he expressed interest in my well-being. There have been many times when he has arranged for our families to be together for a fun event. From shared interests and a common spiritual relationship in Christ, Andy and I have built a deepened level of friendship. Andy has invested in my life and I have gratefully received. Many times, as spiritual leaders, we're all about giving and find it hard to receive. As a pastor's advocate, Andy has invested in me and my life in many ways. I'm grateful for his invitations to be involved in opportunities that help me grow spiritually, in my personal life and relationally with my family. A pastor's advocate is also one who receives. Andy and I have shared times of mutual concern for one another, as well as celebration. We've stood together for many years and because of this, we're both less alone.

Proverbs 17:17 states this, "A friend loves at all times, and a brother is born for a difficult time."

Andy's Final Thoughts

Once Michael and I started our friendship, it didn't take long for me to recognize some similarities in our individual lives. Each time Michael and I met for lunch we continued to build our friendship, I discovered that many of the issues Michael dealt with as a pastor, were very similar to what I experienced in business. The challenges that came with managing 30 employees were similar to the challenges of pastoring a congregation.

Very early in my relationship with Michael, I also recognized that there is a trap into which you can easily fall, if you happen to be a pastor's friend. I must warn you about it. The subtle trap is pride. A pastor's advocate can never have this perspective: "Look at me, look at how important I am because I'm the pastor's advocate." The ministry journey will have many ups and downs. As you go through these events with your pastor, the most effective advocates conduct themselves with humility and display a servant's heart. There's another vital concept you will soon learn in this book. The pastor's advocate is committed to confidentiality and refrains from talking "out of church."

Michael and I have two hopes and prayers with this resource. We hope that if you're a pastor, you will carefully consider the need to find your own pastor advocate. In fact, we want you to pray specifically for a pastor's advocate. We hope that you will carefully look for someone who could serve as your advocate and consider making this invitation. Sometimes, a church leader simply needs a sincere invitation from you, as their pastor, before taking on the role of advocate. It's important to realize that in the beginning, this individual may not be the perfect advocate, but your advocate should be someone in whom you can confidently trust. You'll want to look for someone who is willing to grow into a deep friendship with you, so as to remove the aloneness, discouragement and disillusionment which inevitably comes with pastoral work.

The pastor's advocate is committed to confidentiality...

If you're reading this book as someone who's been asked to become an advocate or is being considered as a pastoral advocate, we hope that you will carefully consider this calling and join the Lord in supporting and encouraging your pastor and his family. It will be a great journey!

INTRODUCTION

Discussion Questions

PASTOR

Have you had an advocate in the past?

Have you had times when you needed an advocate?

Do you have someone in mind for a advocate currently?

ADVOCATE

Have you had an advocate relationship with a Pastor in the past?

Have you had an advocate relationship in other areas of your life?

PRAYERFUL SUGGESTION

For Using This Book As A Resource

Frequent Pastor-Advocate meeting using this book as a resource might include –

- RECAP of personal insights discovered through the chapter.
- CELEBRATING together the chapter's ENCOUNTER WITH JESUS as the pastor and advocate reflect on the Spirit's fresh work of Christ-likeness.
- SHARING a story of the chapter's EXPERIENCING SCRIPTURE as it was practiced with the Lord, with our families and friends, in our vocation and with others who need to know Jesus.
- Spend significant TIME FOCUSED on living out the ENGAGING FELLOWSHIP EXERCISE. Since some of God's light and love is in His people, it will be important for pastors and advocates to spend time completing the 'Engaging Fellowship' sections of the text as they seek to fervently love one another from the heart (1 Peter 1: 22). Becoming more like Jesus is realized when we take the time to truly fellowship with other Jesus-followers.
- Continue to meet over time, complete questions at end of chapters at meetings. Share prayer requests on journal pages after Chapter 6
- CONCLUDE by sharing needs and PRAYING FOR ONE ANOTHER.
- Questions repeat as a discussion guide on page 156.

CHAPTER 1

A Pastor's Friend Lifts the Load of Ministry

Exodus 17:10-12

"Joshua did as Moses said to him, and fought with Amalek: and Moses, Aaron, and Hur went up to the top of the hill. And so it was, when Moses held up his hand, that Israel prevailed: and when he let down his hand, Amalek prevailed. But Moses' hands became heavy, so they took a stone and put it under him and he sat on it. And Aaron and Hur supported his hands, one on one side, and the other on the other side; and his hands were steady until the going down of the sun."

The background of Exodus 17 is that the people of God were coming out of the land of Egypt; God had raised up Moses to be the mighty man who would lead his people to the Promised Land.

On his journey out of Egypt, He led them through the wilderness. In their journeys, they encountered several challenges which came upon them. One of the challenges they faced came up in Rephidim where there was no water (Ex. 17: 1). The second problem that arose was a battle against the people of Amalek (Ex 17: 8). In this case, Moses, as a spiritual leader of God's people, needed a LIFT. Pastors as spiritual leaders are much like Moses - we need a LIFT too. It's sobering to realize that being a pastor is a very dangerous calling. As stated in the Preface, the Pastor Protection Research Study conducted by LifeWay Research reveals that 1 in 3 pastors state that they feel isolated as a pastor.

From this passage of Exodus 17, I would like to point out several observations that relate to the spiritual leadership of pastors; by taking some clues from the ministry of Moses, I would highlight ways that advocates can

LIFT their pastor. The first thing to one's awareness is that spiritual leaders often come under attack. Considering the case of Moses, he faced two battles — an attack from within the Israelites' camp (verses 1-7) and an attack from without, that is, the camp of the Amalekites. In verses 1-7, we note that the people were murmuring and complaining against Moses, even to the point of desiring to stone him because there was no water. In this midst of this crisis, God gave the solution to Moses, telling him to strike a nearby rock, and out of the rock flowed life-giving water. The second attack came against Moses from outside the camp when Amalekites came and fought with Israel in Rephidim (17: 8).

It is noteworthy that immediately after a spiritual high of God miraculously providing water from the rock that there came a "low blow" of the enemy (the Amalekites) fighting against Israel. Spiritual leadership must be aware that following a great victory will come many times of great spiritual struggle with the enemy. 1 Peter 5:8 encourages pastors to be sober and watch for the attacks of the adversary. The Amalekites fought with Israel. Here, the verb tense indicates a repeated action of the Amalekites such that they continuously waged war against Moses and Israel.

There is nothing more discouraging for a pastor than conflicts. Conflicts that occur within the church can take the wind out of his visionary sails. It causes the pastor to be disheartened and discouraged. How can a people who profess to know the Lord of love act with such hatred toward one another and even him? When I was still young in the ministry, I could remember a man in the first church where I served holding up his watch at me while I was preaching; and after the sermon, he stormed out of the church, refusing to shake my hand. That would be quite upsetting to see people act in such an unChristlike so to state.

As if it is not enough for the pastor to face attacks from within the congregation, conflicts with the 'external forces' is now pressing down on the pastor. The forces of darkness are seeking to put out the prophetic light of Biblical preaching from the pulpit. Many adversaries face the pastor these days. We must understand that spiritual leaders face spiritual attacks. The Bible states in Ephesians 6:12 that, "We do not wrestle against flesh and blood but against principalities, against powers, against the rulers of the darkness of this age, against spiritual host of wickedness in the heavenly places."

The Bible also says in 2 Corinthians 2:11 that we should not be ignorant of Satan's devices. Just as we saw in the life of Moses, pastors as spiritual leaders faced two strategic attacks; one came from 'inside' the local church, and the other from outside the church. Church conflict has sadly become normal and inevitable in every local congregation. In a church, there are people who like to criticize the pastor for his preaching, his leadership and even his family. There are people who think that they have the spiritual gift of critiquing their pastor. It is sad when church leaders and deacons see themselves as a board constituted to monitor the pastor so as ensure that he is doing his job.

> *1 Peter 5:8 encourages pastors to be sober and watch for the attacks of the adversary.*

There is nothing more painful for a pastor than internal church conflict. There are also attacks from the outside, which the pastor faces because the role of a spiritual leader is continually leading God's people to enter hostile territories with the Gospel of Jesus Christ. In the midst of conflicts that come from the outside, or spiritual darkness, we have confidence that if "God is for us, who can stand against us?" (Romans 8:31).

AN ENCOUNTER WITH JESUS

Therefore, there is no condemnation for those who are in Christ Jesus. (Romans 8:1).

Who will bring any charge against those whom God has chosen? It is God who justifies. Who is he that condemns? Christ Jesus, who died – more than that, who was raised to life – is at the right hand of God and is also interceding for us. (Romans 8:33-34).

Pastor/Leader:

Do you sometimes feel accused? Have you experienced the rejection or criticism of others? Do you feel others are often judging you or evaluating you?

Or do you, at times, feel that you deserve to be condemned? Is there an area of your life that has gone unconfessed or that repeatedly causes you to struggle?

Are you burdened by the struggles of this world? Are you weary because of the stress of this life? Are you tired of problems or discouraged by affliction?

To everyone who experiences these feelings of accusation or criticism, the Apostle Paul poses the question: "Who will bring any charge against you?" (Romans 8:33). Paul goes on to answer this question with a declaration of truth. He reminds us that there is only One person with the right and power to accuse, criticize, or condemn: "It is God who justifies" (v. 33). Knowing that we might resist such a liberating truth, Paul asks again, "Who is he that condemns?" (v. 34). Again, we read Paul's reminder that there is only One who has the right to condemn us. Only Jesus has the right to and power to judge, but notice what He is doing for those who believe: He is praying for us (v. 34)! The One person who has the right to judge us – is the same One who is interceding on our behalf! This is why the apostle can say, "There is now no condemnation" for us (v. 1). The One who can condemn us is praying for us.

Allow the Holy Spirit to lead you into a personal experience of Romans 8:33-34 as you encounter Jesus.

Close your eyes and imagine the scene of a courtroom. The words Paul uses are legal terms – words that we hear in courtrooms today: "bring charge" and "condemn." Feel the intimidation of your surroundings. Feel the stress and pressure of the legal environment.

Now, using your imagination look around and see the faces of the people who are in the courtroom with you. Imagine that the faces you see in the jury are the people who have been harsh, cruel, critical or judgmental. The people you see staring back at you are the same ones who have neglected you, abandoned you, betrayed and hurt you.

But remember the truth: Only Jesus Christ, the Righteous One has the right to judge and the power to condemn.

As you sit in the courtroom, your attention turns as you hear heavy wooden doors open. Jesus enters the room. You see His flowing robes, sandaled feet and bearded face. And rather than take His place behind the judge's bench, Jesus stands beside you. He slowly eases His arm around your shoulder and gently leads you to join Him. The two of you kneel together in prayer.

You don't notice it at first, but as you pause to listen, you hear Jesus praying. He is praying about the things on your prayer list. He's praying for the needs in your life and the concerns of your heart. Then you hear Him ask, "Where are your accusers?" You raise your head and realize that the courtroom is empty. Everyone one of those faces that were filled with condemnation and judgment are now gone. Each person who brought a charge against you has vanished. Everyone who responded with neglect or abandonment has disappeared. Jesus then proclaims, "Neither do I accuse you."

The only One who can condemn you, prays for you! The only One who is equipped to judge you, doesn't. The Holy One of the Universe prays for you!

Pause now and allow the Holy Spirit to fill your heart with wonder and gratefulness to Jesus. Spend the next few moments allowing Him to plant these truths into your heart and then share your words of thanks:

Thank you, Jesus for your incomparable love. I praise you because of your grace. I'm filled with gratitude because you pray for me, rather than condemn me. I'm thankful that you pray for me, instead of judge me. Lord, I'm especially grateful to you because...

The second important insight that can be learned from this passage is that spiritual leaders inspire and influence people. Notice that Moses, in this battle with Amalekites, stood on the top of a hill with the rod of God in his hand while Joshua and the Israelite army fought in the valley below. When Moses held the rod up, the Bible says that the Israelites prevailed over the Amalekites, but when his hand was let down, Amalek prevailed. It is noteworthy that Moses was standing on the top of a hill with God's rod in his hand. Why would he do that?

Let me suggest a couple of reasons why Moses stood on the top of the hill with the rod of God in his hand. The first reason was that Moses wanted to inspire the people. The rod of God in his hand represented the presence and the power of God over evil. Whenever Moses held that rod in his hands, he was visible to Joshua and the Israelite army that were fighting in the valley at the bottom of the hill. Moses was an inspiration to God's army.

Secondly, that mountain was a place of intercession for the people. On the mountain, Moses was close to heaven, and there he was interceding for the fighters. Do you realize that the greatest influence a pastor can have for his church and community is intercessory prayer? I love what the great Christian missionary, Jim Elliot said, "The saint that advances on his knees never retreats."

Just as Moses' ministry inspired and influenced people, so also a typical pastor being a spiritual leader always inspires and influences people within the church as well as the society. When the pastor gives adequate time to personal devotion in prayer and study of the Word in preparation for his preaching, the entire congregation will be inspired and strengthened. Pastors who are encouraged can become effective leaders who will spiritually lead their congregations to push back depravity and moral decadence in their communities and in the world.

An amazing observation about Moses' ministry is this: spiritual leaders are human! As Moses was holding up the rod in victory, his hands became heavy. Literally, it means that his hands became so tired that he couldn't hold up the staff any longer. It's a very insightful discovery of Moses' leadership — he is human just like every other man on the street. All spiritual leaders, from Moses in the Old Testament to your local pastor today, are human. Sometimes, people tend to place a halo over a pastor's head and treat him as a superhuman person. Do you realize that all pastors as spiritual leaders are human? Pastors today are struggling just like you do. In their 24/7 calling, many pastors are being overworked; they struggle with financial pressures and marital challenges. There's no pastor with an "S" on his chest; he is not Superman with superhuman powers. Pastors have the same needs that every layman has. Therefore, pastors need to be encouraged on a regular basis.

Pastors today are struggling just like you do.

AN EXPERIENCE OF SCRIPTURE

"God, who comforts the downcast, comforted us by the coming of Titus" (2 Corinthians 7:5).

Reflect on this passage for a moment. Here are some of the truths that are captured in this short verse of the Corinthians:

The God of the universe, full of power and strength, apparently chose to use another person to extend His comfort to a weary, spiritual leader. Titus was a trusted follower of Jesus because it had been Titus who was with Paul in his second imprisonment in Rome. Can you imagine the bonding experiences they must have shared in a Roman jail? Titus had also been sent to establish the church at Crete, therefore Titus and Paul shared many things in common: history, struggles, ministry, and their unquenchable faith.

Reflect for a few moments on the unique relationship that must have existed between Paul and Titus.

Now celebrate the blessing of the pastor/advocate relationship and prepare to share your celebrations.

Reflect on a time when God brought a "Titus" into your life to encourage you, comfort you and support you during a time of distress.

I remember a time when God brought ________ into my life. I'm especially grateful for this time and for this person because...

One of the blessings that I've had in ministry is that laymen sometimes take time out of their busy worlds to stop and take a special thought of me. For instance, one layman from my church in Austin loved to write a note to me, and he would put $5 bill in it. He did it every three to four months. In the letter, he would write to share with me how much my ministry meant to him. He would explain to me that when he was in college, his dad who didn't have enough money would send him $5 bill to buy some extra things like sodas or snacks. He then would conclude the note by saying, "Pastor, I don't have much to give, but like my dad I'm going to give you $5 bill just to remind you of my love and appreciation for you." Never forget that pastors are human and that they need your encouragement. Those letters are a source of great encouragement to me to this very day.

Another truth derived from this passage is that spiritual leaders cannot win the battle alone. The Bible states that when Moses' arms became so heavy that he could no longer hold up the rod, two men, Aaron and Hur, came to the aid of Moses. They lifted up his hands until the Israelites won the battle. This is a great discovery as it helps us realize that pastors like Moses need partners to lift up their arms in ministry. Pastors need partners — people like Aaron and Hur that can support and lift their pastor in his times of personal weakness. Spiritual leaders need partners that can be of help and encouragement to their lives and ministry. Philip Yancey said, "I wonder how much more effective our churches would be if we made the pastor's spiritual help, not the pastor's efficiency, our number one priority."

Spiritual leaders need partners that can be of help and encouragement to their lives and ministry.

One with such an Aaron-and-Hur personality is my personal friend and advocate — Andy Spencer. Andy is a layman at Great Hills Baptist church in Austin Texas, where I previously served for six years. Andy has been an encouragement and a LIFTER to me. Many times, when my arms have become weary, Andy's note, word of encouragement or simple lunch appointment provided the strength that I needed to complete the race. These are some of the things that all pastors need and desire from an advocate in their personal life.

These are vital lessons to learn from Exodus 17, as the Bible records the story of the victory that Israel's army had when Moses' weary hands were LIFTED by Aaron and Hur. That act from the two men, Moses' advocates, resulted in triumph for the people of God. The spiritual reality is this: when a pastor is strengthened, the church wins. If a pastor is strong, his ministry will bring about spiritual strength and spiritual maturity within the body of Christ. Sadly, as we look across North America, we don't find many Aarons and Hurs that are lifting up their pastors. I would encourage you to hear the testimony of Andy, and this will serve as a practical application of how he is leading in his local church when it comes to lifting up his pastor.

Could we say that Aaron and Hur were the very first pastor's advocates? Absolutely, "Yes." What does it look like to be a pastor's advocate? The first thing I would say about being a pastor's advocate is that the person would want to motivate his pastor through good advice, a note of thanks, brotherly encouragement, and a good word at the right time. I have come to the realization that these little acts of care from a pastor's advocate necessarily involve little time from the Pastor. It is always great to go to lunch with your pastor, but recognize that it would take some of his time for other ministry schedules. At Great Hills Baptist Church, we came up with a three-part term for what we all should be doing as church leaders. We are there to do three things:

... spiritual leaders cannot win the battle alone.

- Serve our church
- Support our pastor
- Bring unity to the church

This is a universal fact for all lay leaders, deacons, Sunday school teachers, members, committees, and for every layperson. Look at what you're doing around your church and ask yourself, Am I serving my church? Am I providing support to my pastor? Am I bringing unity to the body? If what you're doing as a leader in the church, or even as the pastor's advocate, does not include one of the three things stated above, simply stop doing it. It may not be beneficial to your church.

Encouragement is one of the first things that we need to offer our pastors. When Aaron and Hur lifted his arms, their action was more than just lifting his arms up in the air. It was totally symbolic of their care for Moses. It means that they were standing next to him in battle, and for encouragement in his ministry. I hope that every Gospel minister will be able to raise many, many pastors' advocates across North America and the rest of the world. But then, be ready for attacks, since the evil one does not like a pastor who has a strong advocate. If you're a layperson, recognize the fact that the devil will rise up against you when you take steps to become a pastor's advocate. The devil does not want your pastor to succeed through the help of a good strong advocate. Be ready for that.

Am I serving my church? Am I providing support to my pastor? Am I bringing unity to the body?

As a pastor's advocate, you need to be pure and beneficial to the ministry because your actions in public and in private matter a lot to your life as well as the integrity of your pastor. Our friend Dr. Paul Negrut from Emanuel University in Oradea, Romania, told us recently, "If you do not come face to face with the devil from time to time, you might be walking in the same direction." Sobering words to live by.

A MOMENT OF FELLOWSHIP

"And you are the body of Christ and members individually" (1 Corinthians 12:27).

Reflect on one of your own experiences of interdependence. Then complete the following sentences:

I recall a time when I needed _________ (specify a person's name) and their ___________ (gifts, talents, expertise, advice, counsel, comfort, wisdom or life experience).

The Lord used their (gifts, talents, expertise, etc.) in my life to give __________ (encouragement, comfort, affirmation, etc.) to me.

Share your responses with your pastor or pastor advocate and then together, prayerfully claim the promises of 1 Corinthians 12:25: "That there should be no division in the body, but the members should have the same care for one another."

CHAPTER 1: LIFT LOAD OF MINISTRY

Discussion Questions

Describe your average:

- Day ______
- Week ______

What tasks are most draining (burdensome)?

______

How can we work together to lift the load of ministry?

______

How do you pray?

______

- Daily ______
- Weekly ______

PASTOR

Has there been a time in your ministry when you faced trials?

______

Has there been a time in your ministry when you felt alone and needed an advocate?

______

ADVOCATE

How do you personally serve your Church?

______

How do you personally support your Pastor?

______

Have you ever been attacked for your support of your Pastor?

______

- How? ______
- What did you do to handle it?

  ______

CHAPTER 2

A Pastor's Friend Removes Aloneness from Ministry

Ecclesiastes 4:9-12

"Two are better than one because they have a good return for their work. If one falls down, his friend can help him up, but pity the man who falls and has no one to help him; and also if two lie down together they can keep warm but how can one keep warm alone. Though one may be overpowered, two can defend themselves and a cord of three strands is not quickly broken." (NIV)

The reality is that we must not go about our ministry alone. There was a survey conducted in 2011 by LifeWay Christian Research. It covered a thousand American pastors. The survey revealed that 98% of pastors agreed that they felt privileged to be a pastor, but 55% agreed that they find it easy to get discouraged. Moreover, 55% admitted that pastoral ministry makes them feel lonely at times.

Here, the ancient word of wisdom from Solomon that, "Two people are better than one" has been proven true today. Every pastor needs an advocate in his life. I like how David Apple, in his commentary, states that King Solomon is not primarily speaking about marriage, friendship, partnership or cooperation. He is directly speaking about peer-to-peer relationships such as pastor-to-advocate relationships. This is a great application for our lives, and of course when we look at this text, we find that two are better than one because they have a good reward from their labor. A pastor needs to realize that inviting a friend to come into his life as an advocate would make his ministry more productive. Pastors desire affirmation, appreciation and acknowledgment. We all know and recognize that this will be given at the Judgment Seat of Christ, but it is certainly a joy to pastors' hearts when they receive that on the earth. An advocate can lift his pastor in the lows of ministry.

The Bible says that "two people are better than one because if one falls, the other will LIFT up his companion. Woe to the one who, when he falls, has no one to help him".

It's very interesting that Solomon used an illustration of solitary existence that could arise in travel in those ancient times, comparing the experience to falling into a pit or a deep ravine. We need someone to come along and deliver us out of that. We must realize as pastors that the situation has nothing to do with "if we stumble in ministry," but rather, it's all about those times "when we stumble in ministry". You may be thinking, "I will never stumble in ministry." The Bible has a warning for us in I Corinthians 10:12: "Therefore, let him who thinks he stands take heed unto himself lest he falls." If we fall, and also when we fall, the key to stumbling is a good recovery. Since you want to fall forward, note that the best place to fall is into the encouraging arms of a pastor's advocate, a friend who will help you. I heard a church leader say, "We're all just one moment away from doing something stupid." All it takes is just one look, one word, one text, one attitude, one decision, one action; and from that act, the name of our Lord can be reproached in ministry.

A MOMENT OF FELLOWSHIP

"Don't be so naive and self-confident. You're not exempt. You could fall flat on your face as easily as anyone else. Forget about self-confidence; it's useless. Cultivate God-confidence" (1 Corinthians 10:12 MSG).

Reflect on the times when you may have been naïve or self-confident, only to fall flat on your face. Then consider how circumstances might have been different if you had been able to fall into the arms of a trusted friend. Prepare to talk about this difference with your pastor or advocate.

My naïve perspective or self-confidence got me into trouble when...

Things would've have been much different if ...

In the future, if you see my naïve perspective or over-confidence in the future, I give you permission to call it to my attention. I will receive that feedback from you best as you...

(For example: talk to me privately, reassure me that you care about me first, tell it to me straight and then offer support, etc.)

The pastor's advocate helps LIFT the load of ministry. There is an incredible load that pastors carry in ministry. There is a word in the Japanese vocabulary called "Karoshi"— the word means death from overwork. The syndrome is common in Japan where it claims the life of as many as 30,000 victims every year. Its increase has caused so much concern that since 1990, the Japanese government has been forced to provide restitution for Karoshi widows. We hear this and we think within ourselves, "That's crazy. What are these poor people thinking about?" However, the question is this, when you're overworked, who can speak into your life? Who's your advocate? Can you find a friend whom you can trust in the midst of the burdensome load of ministry? We all go through the hassles of church conflicts and family relationships. During the changing seasons of ministry, where can we go? Only pastors' advocates can lift us when we're pressed down by the load of ministry.

Solomon continues with his illustration in Ecclesiastes 4:11, saying, "When two lie down together, they will keep warm, but how can one be warm alone?" This illustration refers to the journey of travelers in ancient times in the Middle East. Two people would be able to keep warm outdoors in the cold of night. Being alone would add to the load, and the person would need extra blankets. It's good to go on a journey in "twos" so that when, not if, we grow cold in the ministry, there would be someone to LIFT our spirits. This is because pastors often face winter times. There's a wintertime that comes in our personal walk with the Lord; and there can be times when spiritual things become commonplace. There are seasons wherein you might grow cold in your prayer life and your Bible reading habits and thus grow lax in your journey with God.

Without a doubt, spiritual complacency is something we all struggle with in ministry. There can be summertime ministry when God greatly blesses our work, but winter will come when there will be little fruit and merriness. When the cold winter season comes, it's a time to endure and hold on, and it's a time that we really need an advocate to encourage us. Wintertime can come up in a pastor's family in the form of struggles in his marriage, including frustrations and disillusions with his children. Winter can also come in disappointed expectations. What's most important to a pastor in the winter seasons of life and ministry is the graceful role of comrade and friend in an advocate. It's certainly easy to keep up the temperature of life and ministry when we have a friend with a kindred heart walking through difficulties with us. I believe this is one reason why the Lord sent out seventy of His disciples two by two in an evangelism outreach.

A pastor's advocate will LIFT his pastor, thus making the loads of ministry lighter for him to bear. He will encourage him in the winter seasons of ministry; he will give him strength when he is prone to fall in ministry. It's interesting to note that, as a lone pastor, you may be overpowered by an opposing force. If you have a companion, you will be able to withstand the problem, for a "threefold cord is not quickly broken." Now, this is not to say that you'll be overpowered by a burden in your ministry, but you may find yourself at a crossroads where it seems the challenge would overpower you, no matter how spiritual you may be. I'm not saying that you will have adversaries, but when you have one, you will realize the need for an advocate, a true friend that is willing to stand beside you. It's worth noting that there are visible opponents in ministry just like John the beloved talked about Diotrephes, a leader who because of his selfish desire to have prominence in the church, worked against him by speaking malicious words about the apostle

(III John 9). Even the apostle Paul had a problem with Alexander, the coppersmith. These are visible opponents, but there are also invisible opponents.

We see in 1 Peter 5:8 that we should be "sober and vigilant because our adversary walks about like a roaring lion seeking whom he may devour." From this scriptural text, pastors and leaders can take a good clue for their personal life. So it's important that, in the midst of spiritual ambush from opponents, we need an advocate that can stand with us in prayer and in encouragement during such times of struggles. I have heard it said several times that the time to make friends is before you need them. Every pastor is, therefore, encouraged to open up his heart and life so as to have an advocate that can stay with him in the winter seasons, in the overwhelming times that certainly will come in ministry. My advocate for many years now has been Andy, and Andy has an incredible gift when it comes to removing aloneness from a pastor's life.

Pastors desire affirmation, appreciation and acknowledgment.

AN ENCOUNTER WITH JESUS

"But I will send you the Advocate—the Spirit of truth" (John 15:26 NLT).

Every pastor and every church leader can benefit from more encounters with our Advocate – Holy Spirit. The Gospel of John reminds us that the Spirit of truth is with us and actually within us. Pause for moment and consider: The Father loved you so much that He didn't want to leave you without an Advocate. Jesus knew that you would face many of life's struggles and winter seasons of life. Because of His heart for you, Christ sent the Spirit to be your Guide and your Comforter. Jesus couldn't bear the thought of leaving you alone, so He provided an Advocate – One who is always with you because He lives in you!

Prayerfully consider the amazing truth that God cared so much about your aloneness, that He provided an Advocate. Allow the Holy Spirit to speak to you and confirm His presence. Hear His voice of affirmation, encouragement, comfort and support. What does it do to your heart to reflect on these truths?

When I consider that Christ cared about me so much that He provided an Advocate who is always with me and always caring for me, I feel...

My heart is moved with gratitude because...

Both need to understand that his work of ministry is not a game of solitaire. What's a practical way by which a pastor's advocate can be fully ready to remove aloneness from a pastor's life? It's as simple as this: make the call, and take the call. Now what does that mean? There is a country song, "The Call," by Matt Kennon. The theme of the song goes like this: someone was in a crisis in his or her life; and at that moment, the phone rang and he decided to take the call. At the end of the conversation, the person who was at the crossroads of life makes a simple statement, saying, "I'm so glad you called."

Get to a point in your life where you can freely talk about any issue, including critical and important matters.

Make the call; take the call. As a pastor's advocate, if you sense something about your pastor, be ready to make that call. That call may take the form of a text message, an email, or a note delivered to the church office. Whatever it is, be ready to make that call. There may even be times where you need to pay him a visit. Your pastor may just need to go eyeball to eyeball with someone with whom he can discuss his concerns and burdens. So, don't hesitate to call him one way or the other.

Pastors, take the call from your advocate. When he sees your name on his caller ID, unless he's in an absolute emergency, he will also attempt to take your call. Now, can it be a text message that reads, "I will call you right back"? Sure. Can it be a follow-up call? Yes. Make sure that, whenever possible, you will take the call from any advocate that chooses to get in touch with you. Be informed at this moment that your pastor may be only one moment away from a crisis.

As an advocate, you should note that just as your pastor may feel lonely sometimes, his family may also be passing through the valley of loneliness. So, whenever possible, try to include the pastor's family in your activities. We had a great tradition when we were in Austin – we simply called it "Kathy's kitchen." At Andy and Kathy's house, we had wonderful times with our families in Kathy's kitchen, where we enjoyed numerous Sunday nights of fantastic biscuits and gravy. We always had incredible times together. Be sure to include your pastor's family in your acts of care, so as to remove aloneness from his family.

Pastors should endeavor to spend time together with their advocate. Get to a point in your life where you can freely talk about any issue, including critical and important matters. This is a key to ensuring continual and consistent victory over challenges that may come up at each junction of the ministry journey. Soon, in another chapter, you will learn how to talk about important things such as accountability.

Again, I like to caution pastors' advocate that they should be ready for arrows from naysayers. There may be arrows coming from within and without the church. Also, pastors and advocates should be wary of pride. I used to think that pride was something I would never have to deal with, but that it was other people's problem. Looking at things in my life and many crises that I have passed through, how many of them are directly tied up with pride? My own unwillingness to recognize the hidden pride in me hurt me and my ministry.

AN EXPERIENCE WITH SCRIPTURE

"God opposes the proud but gives grace to the humble" (James 4:6 NLT).

One of the best ways to demonstrate humility is to vulnerably admit your need. Prepare for a conversation with your pastor or advocate. Share your responses to the following, demonstrating your humility and allowing the Lord the opportunity to bless your relationship with grace.

You'll know that I need "a call" when ...

(For example: I'm overwhelmed with ministry activities; the kids and my wife are starting school – that's an especially busy time of year; I get short-tempered or critical, etc.)

It's at those times when I need to sense that I'm not alone. I would feel less alone if we could...

(For example: I would feel less alone if we could get together for breakfast once a week; pray together before worship services, plan some fun things to do together as families, etc.)

CHAPTER 2: REMOVE ALONENESS

Discussion Questions

BOTH

Have you ever stumbled in your ministry? ____________________

Have you ever felt overworked in your ministry? ____________________

Have you ever had a friend to aid you in ministry? ____________________

Have you ever taken a "call" to help your Pastor? ____________________

Have you ever had a true accountability partner?

____

Do you recognize and know each other's family?

____

Do you have each other's contact information? ____________________

What does the caller ID say when each calls the other?

____

Do you have a "Kathy's Kitchen" type of place?

____

Does "pride" get in your way? ____________________

- What does "pride" look like for you?

  ____

What does it look like when you are overworked?

____

- Physically?

  ____

- Emotionally?

  ____

CHAPTER 3

A Pastor's Friend is an Encourager

II Corinthians 7: 5-7

"For indeed, when we came to Macedonia, our bodies had no rest, but we were troubled on every side. Outside were conflicts, inside were fears. Nevertheless God, who comforts the downcast, comforted us by the coming of Titus, and not only by his coming, but also by the consolation with which he was comforted in you, when he told us of your earnest desire, your mourning, your zeal for me, so that I rejoiced even more."

Pastors need encouragement, as there are highs and lows that they will always face in their ministry. It's very interesting to note that God is described in the given Bible text above as the God who "comforts the downcast." God offers the ministry of comfort, which is the ministry of coming alongside and giving of strength to an individual. The New Living Translation states it this way: "God encourages those who are discouraged." It's very interesting that the Apostle Paul opened his heart and talked about the pressures that he faced as a spiritual leader. In verse 5, his statement revealed that there is no rest for leaders — this is a confession that shows the reality of what pastors face every day, and it could lead to fatigue for the body. That is, a pastor can become physically exhausted, thus lacking the physical strength to continue his journey.

Many pastors actually admit to feeling guilty for having taken a break.

Many pastors work more than 50 hours a week because of the demands and pressures of ministry. Many pastors are engaged in a myriad of ministry schedules and appointments for weeks without taking a day off, or throughout the year without taking a vacation. Many pastors actually admit to feeling guilty for having taken a break. Zeal and good intention can fuel a pastor's busyness at the beginning, but they won't last through the long haul. The Apostle Paul also confessed that he had some conflicts in ministry both within and without the perimeter of his ministry. Undoubtedly, the apostle faced persecution and opposition everywhere he went; there was a group of hostile, unbelieving Jews that continually instigated troubles against him.

AN ENCOUNTER WITH JESUS

Pause for a few moments and ask the Lord to help you encounter His love in fresh, new ways. The passage above reminds us of the character of God. God comforted the Apostle Paul when his body was weary and when trouble was on every side. God felt compassion when Paul was afraid and when he was surrounded by conflict and turmoil. Reflect on the truth of this passage and what it says about God's response to our struggles. Hebrews 13:8 tells us that Jesus is the "same yesterday, and today and forever." So the same God who felt compassion for the Apostle Paul feels compassion when he sees your weariness. The same God, who comforted Paul when he was afraid and downcast, is the same God wants to comfort you.

First, tell God about any circumstances that are troubling your heart. Pour out your heart before the Lord.

God, at times I am weary of ...

I need you to know that I feel so afraid when ...

God, when I see the conflict around __________, I feel...

I need your help because it seems like there are troubles on every side because...

Now, make the truths of 2 Corinthians 7:5-7 more personal. Imagine that Jesus is standing beside you. His face is full of kindness and understanding. He puts his hand on your shoulder and begins to speak.

"Thank you for pouring out your heart to Me. Just as I comforted my brother, Paul, I want to do the same for you. I know you are weary and often tired. It hurts my heart to see you struggle. I see the times when you are afraid. It's at those times, when I whisper a prayer to the Father, asking Him to give you peace. I too, see the conflict that surrounds you and I feel great compassion. My heart aches when the people I love aren't experiencing unity and love. I hurt with you because of the trouble.

I see the struggles and want you to know that you are not alone. I am the same One who comforted Paul and I long to give that same compassion for you, My Beloved."

Receive these words. Let the God of all comfort, comfort you in this very moment.

Now, pause to give Him thanks.

God, thank you for your compassion. Thank you for loving me and comforting me in my struggles. I'm especially grateful for your compassion because...

The Greek word for conflict refers to military combat or even a sporting contest. Pastors that persevere in the Gospel of Christ and the authority of the Holy Scripture will face opposition, rejection and threats from unbelieving communities around them. Not only did Paul confess to being fatigued from all those conflicts he faced in the course of his journey, he also confessed to insecurity; he said there were fears within. This acknowledges being uncertain or anxious, and even lacking confidence. Paul confessed in II Corinthians 3:5 that he did not feel sufficient of himself or think anything of himself, but that his sufficiency is from God. Insecurity is a feeling that all pastors struggle with, regardless of their education, experience, successes, or failures in ministry. It's important for a pastor's advocate to be aware of this reality, that his pastor may have a feeling of insecurity after a sermon that he has preached very powerfully, and that every Monday morning, his pastor may also feel low. Such feelings frequently come up when a pastor is going through a time of conflict in his local church.

But then, it is amazing that Paul transparently confessed the pressures that he was facing; it's also amazing to understand the way God comforted this great apostle, pastor, and church leader in his generation. The Bible says, according to the words of Paul, that God comforted him through the visit of Titus, and the two of them had a refreshing time together. The God of the universe, who is full of power and strength, chose another vessel to extend his comfort to a weary spiritual leader.

AN EXPERIENCE WITH SCRIPTURE

"Freely you have received, therefore freely give" (Matthew 10:8)

Reflect on the fresh experience of comfort that you have just shared with Jesus. Recall the other times when you have received compassion and care from the Lord. You have freely received comfort from the God. Now, how might you freely give? Ask God to speak:

Pastor: God, you've freely given comfort to me. Who needs some of that same compassion delivered through me?

Pastor Advocate: "God, you've freely given comfort to me. How can I share Your compassion with my pastor? Show me how to comfort in weariness, trouble, conflict or fear. Speak Lord, I want to hear you."

Who is Titus by the way? He is not very well known; we know from a Biblical perspective that he was a Gentile companion with Paul on his missionary journeys. He was one of those who started the church in Crete, he was with Paul on his second missionary journey, and he was even the one who delivered Paul's letter of scathing rebuke to the Corinthian church. God used Titus to comfort Paul when he was low, discouraged and even depressed. This is what we call the "Titus Touch of Encouragement" to pastors.

There is a myth about one King Midas who was very popular with people because his ability usually turned everything he touched into gold. This came to be known as the golden touch or the Midas touch. Titus, by virtue of his coming to Paul and bringing some godly reassurance to him, was the one who brought the golden touch of encouragement to the apostle; he was the one that God used to encourage Paul in his season of utter discouragement.

In view of this, pastors' advocates should know that God takes delight in the ministry of encouraging and strengthening a pastor. Will you join Him to fulfill that purpose? Will you join God in encouraging and lifting your pastor? Let's hear from Andy as he shares some practical ways by which he has extended the Titus Touch.

For those of you that are reading this book as a potential pastor's advocate, I (Andy) have some questions for you: are you feeling overwhelmed yet? Are you wondering in your heart, saying, how in the world can I, a layperson, take on this awesome responsibility as a pastor's advocate? I thought the same way for a long time. It overwhelmed me to realize that I was moving down a path to where my pastor's well-being was entrusted to me. In fact, my pastor trusted me with important aspects of his life. What an awesome responsibility! I felt way under qualified. How in the world could I help my pastor? I recognized quickly that there were some simple things that I could do. The first thing I could do was to constantly pray for him (more details are given on this subject of prayer in Chapter 9). I also recognized another aspect from my business life that was quite important for me as a pastor's advocate. Certain things came to me at a great cost — this has nothing to do with pain, or something physically demanding; this is a great cost in dollars.

What I am about to tell you for the price of this book cost me $20,000. When you are feeling overwhelmed and you are not sure how you are going to be able to help your pastor at a time when there are conflicts in the church, when something heart-breaking has happened inside his life, or when he's not sure where to turn in the midst of confusion, there is something you can do. Over the years, I have learned a very simple question. I call it the $20,000 question. When you're not sure what to do or what to ask your pastor, you should ask this question:

"Can you tell me more about that?"

As pastors' advocates, we may ask this question hundreds of times. Understand that one of the most powerful tools that you can take advantage of in the life a typical pastor is to give him a listening ear. You might not have all the answers; you may not know the answers at that moment, but we all can certainly listen. As we are listening, we might occasionally ask the question, Can you tell me more about that? It's a simple question. It's simply a way for a pastor to dig deeper and think harder about what's going on in his life.

The Titus Touch is the way pastors' advocates can come alongside their pastors and help them with the things going on in their ministry. To help relieve discomfort, fatigue, insecurity and conflict can be as simple as just asking the question:

A MOMENT OF FELLOWSHIP

"...So that through perseverance and the encouragement of the Scriptures we might have hope" (Romans 15:4).

Plan a conversation with your pastor or pastor advocate. Begin your conversation with these words and then listen carefully to one another.

At times, I need God's strength to persevere in...

The Scripture, 2 Corinthians 7:5-7 gives me encouragement because...

God's heart of compassion gives me hope because...

At any time in this conversation, look for opportunities to deepen your understanding of your pastor/pastor advocate by asking:

Can you tell me more about that?

CHAPTER 3: ENCOURAGER

Discussion Questions

PASTOR

Have you faced opposition in your ministry?

From outside?

From inside?

Have you ever felt insecure about your ministry?

ADVOCATE

Do you encourage those around you?

Are you more apt to listen than talk?

Do you use open ended questions often in conversation?

Can you tell me more about that?

What are major stress points in your week?

How do you like to be encouraged?

What makes you feel insecure?

What can you do to be a better listener?

CHAPTER 4

A Pastor's Friend Affirms Pastoral Calling

Hebrews 13:7-8

"Remember your leaders who have spoken God's word to you. As you carefully observe the outcome of their lives, imitate their faith. Jesus Christ is the same yesterday, today and forever."

Hebrews 13 states the importance of pastoral calling. It's written to give the local church a description of what a local pastor offers and what he does. A local pastor is a spiritual leader who leads, guards and oversees a local church. Let me explain each one of these responsibilities.

For a layman, who is a pastor's advocate, you must understand the high spiritual calling that is displayed in your friend's life. He is one who has a great influence upon people both in the church and the society at large. A pastor is called to lead a local church. In the New King James version, Hebrews 13:7 refers to pastors as "those who rule over you, who have spoken the word of God to you, whose faith follow, considering the outcome of their conduct." In verses 7 and 17, a pastor is described as those who rule over you.

The Greek word employed here is not that which refers to reigning as a king or as a governor over a people. The word means "to lead" — it gives the idea of servant leadership, which is taken from our Lord's teaching in Mark 10:45, where Jesus said, "The Son of Man did not come to be served, but to serve, and to give his life a ransom for many" (NKJV). We must be mindful that our Lord modeled spiritual servant leadership when he was found washing the feet of the disciples. What it means to be a leader is to be an influence on people. The Bible says that the faith of the pastor is to be followed. In other words, regarding the outcome of their life, they're living out their faith; and the outcome of our faith is stated in Hebrews 13:8 as "Jesus Christ the same yesterday, today and forever."

As a layperson, you must understand that the church seldom rises above the level of its spiritual leaders. This reality is what drives me to my knees every day before God because I realize that only Christ can give me sufficiency in ministry. This is the reality that should lead every pastor to a deeper devotion to the Word and Christ. As a pastor's advocate, understand the immense load of heaviness that is placed upon a pastor who is called to lead, not only his family but also the entire local church, and to have an impact on the community with the Gospel. The next calling of a pastor, which we find in Hebrews 13, is to feed the local church. In verse 7, the Bible refers to him as one of "those who have spoken God's word to you." How does a pastor lead a local church? It is through the word of God, which is the spiritual food required for raising godly sheep.

The Bible is comprised of the body of messages preached by the early prophets and the disciples and apostles of the Lord. It is the preached Word of God, which is the manna from heaven that can be used to feed the local congregation. So the pastor should devote many hours each week to personal Bible study and preparation. The average time required to prepare for a 30-minute sermon is between 8 and 15 hours. A pastor's advocate should be aware of the responsibility that a local pastor has, which is to hear from God and to speak for God.

Spiritual leaders also guard the local church. The writer of Hebrews says, "Don't be carried about by various and strange doctrines" (13:9). Then, he talks about how we have an altar to which we can run for divine help; it's the altar of the Christ who was crucified outside the gates of Jerusalem. The pastor is called to guard the local church from falling into the mire of false teachings. As a pastor's advocate, understand that there are many media avenues through which people are receiving all kinds of teaching on the Word of God. Encourage your pastor to remain true to the Scripture. Encourage him every time he preaches the Word of God with accuracy and with passion because it is his duty to guard the local church.

In addition, the pastor is called to oversee the local church. Hebrews 13:17 says to pastors: "Keep watch over your souls as those who will give an account, so that they can do this with joy and not with grief, for that would be unprofitable for you." The pastor of a local church is given the responsibility of keeping watch over souls. Literally, the word means to be sleepless or to be watchful. In other words, the spiritual condition of the souls of people within the church and outside the church would always be a thing of great concern for your friend, the pastor. The reason it would give him such concern is because he will give an account of his work on the last Day of Judgment before Christ. Both pastors' advocates and other members of his church should help him do his work of ministry with joy and not with grief.

AN EXPERIENCE WITH SCRIPTURE

"We have placed our confidence in him, and he will continue to rescue us. And you are helping us by praying for us" (2 Corinthians 1:10-11).

Pastor: As you think about these roles of ministry (lead, guard and oversee), which of these might God want to strengthen in you? Ask your advocate, spouse or trusted friend to help you by praying for you.

Share your responses to these sentences and then ask for prayer.

I think God would want to strengthen my leadership by...

I think God might want to strengthen the way I guard our congregation by...

I think God would want to strengthen the way I oversee our church by...

Now, would you pray for me and help me by your prayers?

Pastor Advocate: As you think about these ministry roles (lead, guard, oversee), which of these might God want to strengthen in you – as you relate to your family, ministry leaders, or co-workers? Ask your pastor, spouse or trusted friend to help you by praying for you.

Share your responses to these sentences and then ask for prayer.

I think God would want to strengthen my leadership by...

I think God might want to strengthen the way I guard...

I think God would want to strengthen the way I oversee...

Now, would you pray for me and help me by your prayers?

What creates the greatest joy in the heart of a pastor is to see people respond to the Word of God, know the Word of God, and also grow spiritually. This would bring a happy smile to the pastor's face. On the other hand, overseeing the church under the burden of grief could arise from those that are not responsive to the Word of God, and those that are unwilling to yield everything about their lives to Jesus. This was the sorrow Jesus had when he was moved with compassion for the rich young ruler who turned away from Him because of his riches. It's quite unfortunate that many people have their names on a church membership register, but their names are not written in heaven. There cannot be but sadness in the heart of a pastor if many of his people that confess the truth or are only living a lie. There would be grief in his heart if people claim that they are walking in the light, but have hatred for others and sin in their lives.

More so, a pastor would grieve if he realizes that on the Judgment Day most people who attend church every Sunday will be rejected by Christ who will declare to them, saying, "Depart from me. I never knew you" (Matthew 7:23). As a pastor's advocate, understand the incredible weight that your friend, the local pastor, has — he is there to lead the church, and to oversee the church. His work goes beyond the administration of the church; it deals with the spirituality of souls under his leadership. That's the reason the writer of Hebrews in 13:24 says, "Greet all those who rule over you and all the saints." What does this mean? It means to communicate with your spiritual leader (your pastor) on a regular basis.

The Bible says in I Timothy 5:17 that pastors who labor in the Word are worthy of double honor. It's such an encouraging thing for a pastor to hear you say, "I love you," or "I appreciate you." The role of the pastor is not just preaching a sermon on Sunday, but rather it's living out God's fullness in his daily life. As a pastor's advocate, understand that very well. When his pastoral calling is affirmed through kind words, he will be encouraged. Since Andy has done that for many years in my life, he's going to share how he has affirmed my role as a pastor in our relationship, and in relationships he has had with other pastors.

I (Andy) have found that our pastors, at some point in their lives, felt an absolute calling to the ministry — a calling from God to serve the church as a pastor. Well, many of us who are laypersons may not have felt that calling; we may not even know what that calling looks like. I want to share with you a concept that has greatly changed my life. I call it "Success to Significance." So many of us may not have felt a calling to be pastors; we may have felt a calling to pursue a career in marketing, teaching, nursing, or engineering. How can we use our skills and talents for greater good? Success to Significance, by principle, often takes a look at the skills you have. What are the skills that you have learned? The skills could be inborn ones, and could also refer to the ones you've acquired through personal efforts, for example carpentry and landscaping. How were you able to maximize your skills to bring about success in your life? Have any of your skills added value to the livelihood of your family?

... the church seldom rises above the level of its spiritual leaders.

What does success look like? Having had success and some level of financial success, how do you think you can maximize those skills and take them to the level of significance in a local church? There may be a lot of questions you need to ask yourself, if you really want to become a help to a spiritual leader. What am I passionate about? What do I really love doing? What is that cause that I want to see move forward? Even though you may be an accountant, a nurse, a doctor, or a landscaper in your professional career, there is a way you can leverage on your profession and the resultant riches so as to reach the world for Christ by becoming a pastor's advocate.

Your skills can be incorporated into the fabric of a local church and support the pastorate; and from success, you will attain the realm of significance as far as God's cause is concerned in that church. Many of you may have learned about spiritual gifts; use your study on spiritual gifts in order to unearth what God has given you in addition to your scholastic or non-scholastic skills. Generally speaking, spiritual gifts are supernatural gifts from God, and these include teaching, exhorting leading, mercy, giving, and prophecy. These and many more gifts can enable you to serve as a helping hand to your pastor in his calling.

For instance, my spiritual gift revolves around administration and giving. When I first learned about being a pastor's advocate, I recognized that I was needed by my pastor. While I was in the business world, I was in charge of a company that had 30 staff members. Michael (my pastor) needed some help in administration, as that might not be one of his spiritual gifts. This seemed to be the juncture where we first connected with one another; I was able to offer some help in my process of becoming a pastor's advocate. I would strongly encourage you to discover your calling as a pastor's advocate and affirm your pastor in his calling. Also, identify your skills and spiritual gifts, for they will aid you in this journey of becoming a pastor's advocate and help you move from success to significance.

When his pastoral calling is affirmed through kind words, he will be encouraged.

A MOMENT OF FELLOWSHIP

"So then, just as you received Christ Jesus as Lord, continue to live in him" (Colossians 2:6 NASB).

Reflect on your encounter with Jesus above. In what ways did you yield to the leading of Jesus? In what areas, did you sense a need to learn from him? Talk about these insights with your pastor/pastor advocate.

I need to learn more about leading/guarding/overseeing from Jesus, especially in the area of...

I sense that He wants me to become more __________ (bold, courageous, loving, gentle, forgiving, accepting, discerning, etc.) I know that I'll only learn this from Him.

AN ENCOUNTER WITH JESUS

"Take my yoke upon you and learn of me, for I am gentle and humble" (Matthew 11:29).

Imagine Christ standing before you. His eyes are kind and gentle. His expression is loving and welcoming. As you look more closely, you notice that Christ is wearing a yoke – a yoke of service and love. The purpose of this yoke is to allow the One who is experienced to train another. Jesus stands before you wearing the yoke, and the other side of the yoke is empty. You realize that Jesus is inviting you to join him in loving, leading and serving others well. He is the master teacher and the humble servant who can train, equip, and guide you. Listen to His words:

"Take my yoke upon you and learn from me. I am a gentle and humble teacher who can help you as you lead, guard and oversee the ones whom I have entrusted into your care. Come and take the other side of the yoke and together, we can love your near ones well! Come to me and learn what I know about the people you lead. Learn from me how to guard and protect. Learn from me how to guide and oversee the precious people around you.

Pause in prayer. Tell Jesus about your willingness to join Him in the yoke and learn from him.

Lord Jesus, I do want to join you in better loving and leading...

I yield myself to you. I do want to learn from you, especially how to...

Thank you for sharing this burden and showing me how to...

CHAPTER 4: CALL TO MINISTRY

Discussion Questions

PASTOR

Describe your call to ministry

Describe your sermon prep

Daily

Hour commitment

BOTH

What are your skills?

Passions?

How can they be used together?

What are your top 3 spiritual gifts?

RESOURCE LINK (SPIRITUAL GIFTS INVENTORY FROM LIFEWAY):
http://www.lifeway.com/lwc/files/lwcF_MYCS_030526_Spiritual_Gifts_Survey.pdf

CHAPTER 5

A Pastor's Friend Encourages Transparency

II Corinthians 3:18

"But we all, with unveiled face, beholding as in a mirror the glory of the Lord, are being transformed into the same image from glory to glory, just as by the Spirit of the Lord."

In II Corinthians 3, attention is drawn to the authentic transparency of the Apostle Paul as a shepherd leader. If there was ever a great pastor and an effective spiritual leader, Paul would be placed in such a classification. By the power of God's will, his life was transformed from being a persecutor to being a preacher. God used Paul to rapidly spread the Gospel through the world. As you read through the New Testament, you would find out that he wrote over 1/3 of the books in the New Testament. Some of his confessions showed that he was sometimes vulnerable to limitations that tended to discredit the integrity of his ministry. That was why he was very transparent about who he was and what his challenges were — he didn't pretend as if all was well with him. Growing as a spiritual leader often brings some vulnerability if you are the lone minister in your local church. Therefore, you must learn to be open in your confessions before the Lord, and even to a pastor friend or an advocate in whom you can confide.

It is a sign of healthy maturity when a leader desires to grow and to develop in his spiritual journey with people. The reality of the ministry starts when a pastor graduates from a Bible college or a seminary; he shouldn't think that he has come to the end of growing in his spiritual relationship with the Lord. Reading through II Corinthians 3, you can find out for yourself the real mind and heart of a great pastor. Paul's confession attests to the fact that an effective pastor knows his own needs, limits and shortcomings, and these will always prompt him to seek God's help.

Consider the confessions that Paul made in his letter to the church at Corinth. As a pastor's advocate, allow these confessions to move your heart with compassion toward lifting your pastor by your acts of prayer and care. Similarly, if you're a shepherd, you should take a clue from the first confession Paul made by saying:

"I genuinely care for you."

In II Corinthians 3:2, Paul says to the local church: "You, yourselves are our letter written on our heart, recognized and read by everyone." Here, Paul is speaking about commendations in ministry. Paul clearly stated that his commendation was his relationship with the people at Corinth based on the Gospel. The only commendation that Paul desired is that his life had been transformed by his Gospel ministry. But then, take note of his transparency when he said to the people that they were his commendation — the proof of his ministry. I believe that it is the desire of your pastor to be known as someone who cares for you. As an advocate, take time write a letter, send an e-mail message, or use social media to express your gratitude for the caring heart of your pastor. Your words of affirmation and appreciation will strengthen your pastor as he runs the Christian race and performs his ministry schedules.

...that an effective pastor knows his own needs, limits and shortcomings...

Let's take a look into the next confession of Paul:

"My adequacy is from God alone."

In II Corinthians 3:5, he stated, "It is not that we are confident in ourselves to consider anything as coming from ourselves, but our confidence is from God." (HCSB) Confidence means sufficiency; adequately feeling fresh and effective. It is God who enables the pastor to perform his ministry task; it is God who can make him sufficient for the task. Paul's confidence didn't come from his theological training; neither did it come from his years of ministry experience. Also, it didn't come from the people that he knew in his time. Rather, his confidence for the Gospel ministry came from God. God made him confident as a minister of the new covenant.

Realize that when God wants to save a man, He will save him in the time of his desperate need. In ministry, God continually keeps us at every point of desperation, and we should be totally dependent on Him. If Apostle Paul, a great pastor and leader in the early church, could confess that his adequacy was in Christ alone, then it wouldn't be strange if your pastor makes similar confessions at different points in the course of his journey.

AN ENCOUNTER WITH JESUS

"For the LORD... takes the upright into his confidence" (Proverbs 3:32 NIV).

Reflect on the times when you have sensed that the Lord has taken you into His confidence? When has he shared special insights with you? When have you heard from the Lord during your times of prayer, study or reading of Scriptures? When has God revealed himself or his plans through another believer or moment of worship?

I remember having a personal encounter with Jesus, when he took me into his confidence and...

- drew me close to him by...
- gave me specific direction about...
- provided a warning about...
- revealed more of himself as...
- confirmed that...
- affirmed me for...
- reassured me that...

Ask the Holy Spirit to help you remember the times when the Lord has revealed himself to you in these ways. Allow God to renew your confidence. Remember that it is the God of all creation who has taken you into his confidence. Let him confirm your calling and purpose, then thank him in prayer. Let your confidence come from God.

God, thank you for revealing yourself to me. I stand sufficient and confident in your calling because of who you are and what you have done.

I must say that, in spite of my 27 years of serving as a minister in local churches, I still feel inadequate regarding the great task of handling the Word of God and shepherding a local church. I love the story told about C. H. Spurgeon. Do you know that several times Spurgeon would sit late at night to study and prepare a message? Still, in many cases, he couldn't complete his sermon. There are times that he would go to church and walk all the way to the pulpit with no prepared sermon. He would have to believe God for some divine help to speak the Word under the unction of the Spirit. It was a practice of Spurgeon as he walked into the pulpit to pray this way: "I believe in the Holy Spirit. I believe in the Holy Spirit. I believe in the Holy Spirit." This makes it obvious that pastors need the prayer and support of God's followers. So, I would like to encourage you as a pastor's advocate to take some time daily to pray for your pastor and his family. Motivate him so that you can see God working in his life and increase his adequacy.

Pray that God keeps your pastor close to Him and that he should keep him pure in mind and heart as he walks with Him. Now, let's consider the third confession of Apostle Paul:

"I want to administer life in the Spirit."

Paul stated in II Corinthians 3:7 that "Now if the ministry of death, chiseled in letters on stones, came with glory, so that the Israelites were not able to look directly at Moses' face because of the glory from his face—a fading glory— how will the ministry of the Spirit not be more glorious? For if the ministry of condemnation had glory, the ministry of righteousness overflows with even more glory." (HCSB) The background of this text is the giving of the Law on Mount Sinai which came with a glorious experience as the mountain was filled with smoke, fire and quaking. After Moses had received the Law and came down from that mountain, his face radiated a light of glory before the people.

The Bible states in Exodus 34:29 that Moses didn't know that the skin of his face was shining while he was talking with God who gave him the tablets of the Law. Notice the argument — if this law was given with fading glory to Moses, how much more will the Gospel be even more glorious. And, it states also that the ministry of the Spirit will not fail to be more glorious. The application is that spiritual leadership must be characterized by opportunities to hear from heaven for the good of the congregation. So, the church should learn to give pastors adequate seasons of study times; give pastors adequate time for sermon preparation and uninterrupted prayers because they need to hear from God each week.

In Acts 6:4, the Bible has a record of the lifestyle of the early church leaders who said: "We will devote ourselves to prayer and to the preaching ministry." Pastors' advocates should encourage their leaders to give themselves to a quality time of study and prayer. It's worth noting that the average preparation time for a 30-minute sermon is anywhere between 8 and 15 hours a week. Some pastors may even require more than others. Yet, the reality is that all pastors need seasons of quiet study each week. As a pastor's advocate, keep in mind that if your pastor is always available to you, he will not be effective when it comes to the time you need him to speak God's word to your heart.

Paul's fourth confession reveals a great puzzle in the chapter under consideration:

"I desired to preach with boldness."

He stated this in II Corinthians 3:12, saying, "Therefore, having such a hope, we use great boldness." (HCSB) Every pastor has the desire to preach with boldness of speech. I must confess and reflect, as a pastor, that all pastors would be inclined toward this simple truth, that we all need boldness. No pastor can preach the word without boldness. In order to share the truth of the Gospel with people, we all need to do a fresh turning to the Lord in our life. Pray that boldness will be given to you whenever you preach in your local church. Pastors' advocates should also include this in their prayers for the pastor of their local church. Also, occasionally after the service, walk up to your pastor to encourage him each time he speaks the Word of God boldly behind that pulpit!

Pray for your pastor that God will grant him deeper spiritual experiences with Christ in His word. The Apostle Paul's fifth confession is very significant:

"I am on a Christ-likeness journey with you."

In the last verse of that II Corinthians 3:18, Paul stated, saying, "We all with unveiled faces are looking as in a mirror at the glory of the Lord, and we are being transformed into the same image from glory to glory. This is from the Lord who is a Spirit." (HCSB) He used the phrase "we all" —

this suggests that he himself was not excluded. Pastor Paul also needed spiritual transformation or growth. As a pastor's advocate, understand that your pastor is growing spiritually along with you. And, his day-to-day experience could be spelled as PBPWMGINFWMY, or "Please be patient with me, God is not finished with me yet." Paul confessed that he was being changed and transformed along with the local church. If you're a pastor, and you are not being spiritually transformed, the church will not experience spiritual transformation.

AN EXPERIENCE WITH SCRIPTURE

"Search me, O God, and know my heart; test me and know my anxious thoughts. See if there is any offensive way in me, and lead me in the way everlasting" (Psalm 139:23-24 NASB).

Be still before the Lord and make the same request of Psalm 139. Ask God to search your heart and identify any parts of your life that need to be changed in order to see more and more Christ-likeness. Your prayers might begin like these:

Search me, O God, and show me the sins that hinder me from becoming more like you. Free me from anything that's immoral or evil. Free me from any malice, deceit, hypocrisy, envy or slander. I want to have a clean mind and heart, so show me anything about my life that needs to change.

Search me, O God, for unresolved emotions. Free me from any guilt or condemnation, any anger or bitterness, any fear or anxiety. Free me to live each moment "in the present" with you. What parts of my emotions need to change?

Search me, O God, for any childish things that distract me from becoming more like you. Free me from rationalizing my behavior and blaming others. Free me from idle chatter and self-focus. Help me to practice personal responsibility before you and others. What are the childish things that need to be put away?

Search me, O God, for areas of self-reliance that prevent me from becoming more Christ-like. Free me from my thoughts, my ways, my ideas and my goals. I want to embrace Your thoughts, Your ways, Your ideas and Your goals. Show me any ways that I am putting my plans above Yours.

Pause and wait for the Lord to speak to you about one or more of these areas. Then yield to him, even though you may not know all that will be necessary for change and Christ-likeness. Pray a prayer of yieldedness.

Lord, I sense the need to put away __________ from my life. Even though I don't know all that this change will require, I yield to You. Remove this from my life so that I can become more and more like You.

A spiritual leader can only lead a church as far as he himself is growing spiritually in his walk with the Lord. Therefore, I encourage every pastor's advocate to embrace his pastor as a fellow pilgrim on this journey of growing in Christ-likeness, for the journey will not end until we see our Lord face to face. Once again, let's go over the confessions that Paul made in his letter to the Corinthian church as recorded in II Corinthians chapter 3:

1st confession: I genuinely care for you.
2nd confession: I desire my adequacy to come from God alone.
3rd confession: I want to minister life in the Spirit.
4th confession: I have the desire to preach with boldness.
5th confession: I am on a Christ-likeness journey with you.

Endeavor to lift up your pastor by encouraging transparency in his personal life. How important is faithfulness in prayer for your pastor? Dr. Wilbert Chapman often told of an experience as a young man when he went to become a pastor of a church in Philadelphia. After his first sermon, an older gentleman said to him, "You are pretty young. You are pretty young to be a pastor of this church, but you preach the Gospel, and I am going to help you all I can." Dr. Chapman thought he was a crank, but the man continued, saying, "I am going to pray for you that you may have the Holy Spirit's power upon you. Two others have covenanted to join me and pray for you." Dr Chapman said he didn't feel so bad when he learned that the old man was going to pray for him.

Thereafter, the three men became ten, the ten became twenty, the twenty became fifty, and the fifty became two hundred. The group usually met before every service to pray that the Holy Spirit might come upon Dr. Chapman. He said, "I always went into the pulpit feeling that I would have the answer to the prayers of those who had faithfully prayed for me. It was a joy to see the result as we received one thousand one hundred people into our church by conversion in just three years. Most of them were men. It was the fruit of the Holy Spirit and answer to prayer."

Encourage and allow your pastor to be transparent and real with you in your relationship together. It's important for the two of you to have honest conversations together. Pastors need to be open to that type of friendship, though this concept of transparency may be something that you have not experienced. It's a level of accountability you can express to each other. Andy contributed to my transparent lifestyle as a pastor.

I (Andy) love the message that Michael has just brought up in this chapter, even as he provides some insight into the five confessions of Pastor Paul. These five areas in a pastor's life are very important as we all we need to work on our transparency through mutual openness that would make us feel free to ask each other tough questions. We might even call them "accountability questions." That is, questions that will cover these five critical areas in the life of a pastor. In your relationship with your pastor and his family, we can start to develop some accountability and transparency questions.

Nothing is more important than spending time with your pastor or with your advocate in an atmosphere where you can be authentic with each other.

You don't have to feel like you need to schedule an appointment with him to ask those questions. Be natural. Just initiate a conversation and logically ask a question on one area of the confession. For instance, when you go for lunch and you're talking about family life, you may ask him, saying, "Did you go to the theater with your wife this week? I know that your wife likes to go to movies." Michael has asked me often, "Did you play scrabble with your wife this week?" He knows that my wife loves to play scrabble. A question like that could be the starting point of an honest conversation. Appendix 1 provides you with a great list of accountability questions.

The questions came to us from a pastor, Hank Williams (not the singer Hank Williams). He is from Boiling Springs, South Carolina. Hank is a pastor that has taken time to invest in accountability and transparency. He has a list of questions that his accountability partner, his friend and advocate, asks him on a weekly basis. Take note that this concept is also a two-way street since the pastor himself may ask the same kinds of questions, and this could become a great conversation. More so, the questions cut across a wide variety of issues, especially in personal life, family and ministry. In effect, both of you will be developing a more effective ministry.

As much as possible, these key questions should be asked in a conversational format, and honesty should be maintained in every way. Nothing is more important than spending time with your pastor or with your advocate in an atmosphere where you can be authentic with each other. Understand that there are many pressures in ministry and we need to have a reliable person that we can talk to. Some pastors don't necessarily like the word accountability, because it sounds as if it's a business partnership or a legalistic relationship. We don't have to use that term. Transparency could be a better word to use. It's all about spending time together to talk about the real things in our lives.

A MOMENT OF FELLOWSHIP

"Because we loved you so much, we were delighted to share with you not only the gospel of God but our lives as well" (1 Thessalonians 2:8).

Plan a time with your pastor/pastor advocate and share your responses to the following. Let this be a time of sharing the story of your lives together.

I've had these conversations with Jesus lately...

I've heard the Lord say...

As I reflect on my relationship with my spouse (or closest friends if not married), and I feel...

When I think about my relationship with my kids (if applicable), I feel ______ because...

My greatest celebration within ministry right now is...

My greatest challenge in ministry right now is...

CHAPTER 5: TRANSPARENCY

Discussion Questions

What are you transparent about?

What do you need to be more transparent about?

Are there any confessions you need to make today?

Do you have a "quiet place" to study?

How can you protect that place?

How and what can I (should I) hold you accountable for?

CHAPTER 6

A Pastor's Friend Prays for Him

Ephesians 6:18-20

"Pray at all times in the Spirit with every prayer and request, and stay alert in this with all perseverance and intercession for all the saints. Pray also for me, that the message may be given to me when I open my mouth to make known with boldness the mystery of the Gospel. For this I am an ambassador in chains. Pray that I may be bold enough in Him to speak as I should."

A pastor's friend is his greatest intercessor. Going through Paul's letters, it is very important to notice that several times Paul, an apostle and pastor, implored others to pray for him. In Ephesians 6, Pastor Paul's words reveal that the believers' prayer is urgently needed by their pastor, whom God has called as the leader of God's people. He once said to the brethren — "Now I beg you, brethren, through the Lord Jesus Christ, and through the love of the Spirit, that you should strive together with me in prayers to God for me" (Romans 15:30).

In Colossians 4:3-4, Paul wrote to the Colossians that they should be fervent in "praying for us that God would open unto us a door for the word, to speak the mystery of Christ, for which I am also in chains, that I may make it manifest, as I ought to speak." To the Thessalonians, he strongly beseeched them, saying, "Brethren, pray for us." (I Thessalonians 5:25). Paul called on the Corinthian church to offer some spiritual help to his ministry by praying — "You also helping together in prayer for us" (II Corinthians 1:11). This was to be part of their work. The believers were always encouraged to help him though intercession. In addition, in his closing word to the Thessalonian church about the importance and necessity of their prayers, he stated, "Pray for us, that the Word of the Lord may run swiftly and be glorified, just as it is with you, and that we may be delivered from unreasonable and wicked men." (II Thessalonians 3:1).

AN EXPERIENCE WITH SCRIPTURE

"Pray for us. Pray that the Lord's message will spread rapidly and be honored wherever it goes..." (II Thessalonians 3:1 NLT).

Pause now and do the Book, take the time to actually be a "doer" of the Word. If you are a pastor's advocate, pause and pray for your pastor right now. If you are a pastor, take this time to pray for one of your fellow ministers. Pray for another pastor's life and ministry.

Pray for the concerns of the pastor's heart and ministry. If you don't know specifics, ask the Lord for wisdom in what to pray. Then, pray that God's message, delivered through your pastor, will spread rapidly and will be honored among believers and lived out with passion.

God, I want to pray for ______.

Please strengthen my friend's personal/family life by...

Strengthen my friend's ministry by...

I ask You to give my pastor boldness to preach Your message and that this message would spread rapidly among our congregation and community. Help us live out Your truth, so that we bring honor to You.

Paul also informed the Thessalonians of the fact that all his opposition can be made inferior to the power of the Gospel through the strength of their prayers for his ministry. A great man of God, E. M. Bounds, said, "The praying ones are to the preacher as Aaron and Hur were to Moses. They hold up his hands and decide the issue that is so fiercely raging around them."

Every pastor needs support and encouragement through the prayer of a pastor's advocate. The pressures of ministry are too great to describe. To learn wisdom, just consider the plight of the Apostle Paul, the greatest pastor who ever lived.

The Apostle Paul confessed in II Corinthians 1:8 that he was so burdened with the loads of ministry that he despaired of life. If Paul could experience that, your pastor will always experience the stress and the strain of daily ministry. The greatest support that pastors' advocates can give to their pastor in the overwhelming flood of stressful demands of ministry is to pray continually for him. Pray for your pastor and send text messages to him often and more often. Encourage a group of other church members and leaders to take up the challenge of serving as intercessors for him and his family. Pray for him at the early hours of Sunday morning, and send him a text that you're praying and eagerly waiting for the message of the day. Pray about specific needs in his life. Gather around him on the Lord's Day and pray for him as he preaches God's Word with power. Take him out for lunch and share with him your support and your desire to be his friend. Invite he and his family to spend time with your family. Pray for your pastor with no hidden agenda. Love him and his family with the love of God.

Pray for your pastor...

A MOMENT OF FELLOWSHIP

"...I urge you in the name of our Lord Jesus Christ to join in my struggle by praying to God for me. Do this because of your love for me, given to you by the Holy Spirit" (Romans 15:30 NLT).

As the pastor's advocate, reflect on a few church leaders who might join you in the calling of praying for your pastor. Ask these individuals to be a part of a team of leaders who lift up your pastor in prayer.

Pastor, ask yourself: "Who would I like to join me in the struggles of ministry? Who should be a part of the team that prays for me?" Ask these individuals to be a part of a team who lifts you up in prayer.

Ask the Lord for wisdom and then write the names He gives you here:

Along with this prayer team, make specific plans for prayer: before services, at holiday seasons, during conflict, for a pastor's marriage and family, at a specific time of day or week.

One of the aims of this book is to motivate thousands of believers in Christ to become pastors' advocates, and who on a continual basis, will see the need to pray for their pastor. While I was serving in Austin, one of the men that God placed in my life as a strong prayer support for my ministry and family was Andy Spencer. Andy continues to do the same for many pastors. It's important to recognize that members of a local church should pray for their pastor. There's nothing more important than praying for pastors. You can pray for your pastor when you're with him, or while having a personal time of prayer.

I (Andy) can't actually imagine the number of times in my relationship with Michael wherein we came to a time when we looked at each other and said, "Let's pray; let's pray over this." There was nothing more important that I could do for him than to pray for his success. Pray for your pastor that God would give him strength as he daily comes into contact with the community through his ministry. Pray for your pastor daily that God would help him have a rich time of study and preparation for his upcoming sermon delivery. Pray for your pastor that the Lord will help him to practice what he preaches because a lost world is watching him. The church world is also watching him closely. In addition, pray that he will be able to preach the entire and correct Word of God without fear. From a practical perspective, you may come together right before the service. Typically, praying together may draw the attention of other men who might want to come along too.

Pray for your pastor that God would give him strength...

All lay-leaders in the church should begin to see the need to be engaged in intercession for their pastors. This could be achieved through regular collective prayer gatherings. As for my current pastor, we usually have a special time to pray for him — the pastor will be on his knees or sit on a chair at the center of our prayer ring. We'll stand around him to pray for him. Nothing can be more meaningful than that! Interceding for your pastor is the most important thing that you can do for your pastor as his advocate.

Advocate I would be remiss if I did not take this time to make sure that you "know that you know that you know" that Jesus Christ is your Savior. If you have never prayed to Jesus Christ to be your personal savior, please consider doing that right now. This simple prayer from the Billy Graham Association is a great way to come to know Jesus Christ as your Savior

"Dear God,

I know I'm a sinner, and I ask for your forgiveness.

I believe Jesus Christ is Your Son. I believe that He died for my sin and that you raised Him to life.

I want to trust Him as my Savior and follow Him as Lord, from this day forward.

Guide my life and help me to do your will.

I pray this in the name of Jesus. Amen"

If you just prayed this prayer, meet with your Pastor to discuss your decision.

AN ENCOUNTER WITH JESUS

"He always lives to intercede for them" (Hebrews 7:25).

There were many times when the disciples watched Jesus move to a private place and pray. Christ modeled the importance of prayer. Prayer was the lifeline of the Savior while he was here on earth. Prayer connected the Father with the Son.

If we know that prayer is so important, why do we often struggle to pray? Could it be that we've missed a relational connection of prayer? Spend the next few moments asking the Lord for a renewed perspective on prayer.

The writer of Hebrews tells us that Jesus is still modeling the importance of prayer. In fact, Scripture reminds us that he lives to intercede for us. Pause and reflect for a few moments on the personal truth of this passage. You have a Savior who is praying for you!

Imagine a scene that's similar to the story in the Garden of Gethsemane. Jesus comes to the garden with his disciples. He asks them to wait while he kneels nearby in prayer. Imagine that, on this day, you are one of those disciples. After some time, you leave the others and walk toward the place where Jesus is praying. You hear him talking to the Father, but can't quite make out what he is saying. As you quietly approach, you hear Jesus praying...and he is praying for the needs of your life. He is interceding for the concerns of your heart and pleading to the Father on your behalf. Jesus is praying for you!

What does it do to your heart to know that Jesus, your Savior and your Lord, loves you so much that he is interceding for you? Tell him now:

Jesus, when I consider that you are praying for me – for the needs of my life and the concerns of my heart – I feel...

Now that you have a fresh view of our Savior and how he intercedes for you, how might that impact your desire to pray? Talk to Jesus about your renewed desire to join him in prayer.

Jesus, I am reminded of how you are always praying for me, interceding for me and talking to the Father on my behalf, and that makes me want to...

CHAPTER 6: PRAYER

Discussion Questions

Do you pray daily for your Church?

Do you pray daily for your advocate?

Do you pray daily for your Pastor?

PASTOR PRAYER REQUESTS

ADVOCATE PRAYER REQUESTS

CHAPTER 7

A Pastor's Friend Provides Rest

Mark 6:31

"Jesus said to His disciples, 'Come away by yourselves to a remote place and rest for a while.'"

We have come to a subject that pastors would like to talk about — a new ministry strategy called REST. By having some deep and devotional meditation on this simple term every year, I usually get convicted that local church pastors are not obeying the Lord in the practice of this Sabbath principle. Of course, there are several Scriptural references on the Sabbath, but I just want to highlight and bring certain things to your attention about it. The Sabbath is a scheduled time of spiritual rest for the purpose of ensuring a pastor's spiritual refreshment and relational renewal. Unfortunately, many pastors don't observe this Sabbath in their ministry.

Pastoral ministry is a 24/7 occupation, it can be emotionally, mentally, physically and spiritually taxing. The pace of life, the demands of counseling, public speaking engagements, the strain of leadership, and spiritual warfare can drain our resources. As of today, burnout tendencies are rarely discussed among spiritual leaders because we all feel that we must have it all together and put on a happy face. No one wants to admit that he is feeling weary from his everyday challenges of ministry. Many pastors are hitting the wall of spiritual, emotional and relational burnout.

Pastoral ministry is a 24/7 occupation.

In the book, Soul Keeping, author John Ortberg shares a story about a traveler visiting Africa who engaged a group of carriers and guides with the hope of making her journey a swift one. She was pleased with the progress of the many miles that they covered on the first day. On the second day, all the carriers that she hired remained seated as they refused to move. She was greatly frustrated and asked the leader of her hired hands why they didn't want to continue on the journey. He told her that on the first day they had traveled too far and too fast, and now they were waiting for their souls to catch up with their bodies.

This worldly and hurried lifestyle that most of us live, does for us what that first day's march did for those poor jungle tribesmen. The difference is that they knew what they needed to do to restore life's balance. Too often, we do not. Have you ever felt that you needed the time and space to let your soul catch up with your body? That is a good indication that you need that rest.

Let's consider the new ministry strategy called REST. In the given Bible text above, we could see that Jesus gave importance to rest from the day's ministry journey. I love what Vance Havner wrote about this verse. He said, "If you don't come apart for awhile, then you will come apart in a while." Notice the context of Mark 6:1-5; we find out that Jesus has been rejected in Nazareth, his hometown. In verses 7-13, twelve disciples had been sent out and they experienced the supernatural power of God. Then, in verses 14-29, John the Baptist was beheaded to the shock and dismay of the disciples. In verses 30-32, we find out that the disciples gathered around Jesus and told him all things about their journey, including what they had done and what they had taught. After listening to their testimonies, Jesus said to them, "'Come away by yourselves to a remote place and rest for a while.' For many people were coming and going, and they did not even have time to eat. So they went away in the boat by themselves to a remote place."

It is very important that you prioritize your own rest...

When was the last time you set apart a day to rest and be renewed in your relationship with Jesus and also spend time with your closest loved ones, your wife and your family? It is very important that you prioritize your own rest and refreshment; if you don't, then no one else will. For this, pastors' advocates should make sure that they give their pastor some opportunity to rest whenever it's necessary. Leaders should respond to this invitation from Jesus about the need to rest in each area of their life.

AN EXPERIENCE WITH SCRIPTURE

"Come away by yourselves to a remote place and rest for a while" (Mark 6:31).

Spend an hour alone with the Lord. This isn't the time for Bible study or sermon preparation. This is just a time for you to go away to a remote place and be with Jesus. After you have quieted your heart, ask the Savior to reveal areas of life where He longs to give you rest.

Jesus, I know that I am weary of...

I am burdened because...

In what ways do you want to give me rest? Speak Lord, I'm listening...

Here are practical ways to live out the principle of Sabbath and rest.

1. Take some rest at least one hour every day. This was the habit of our Lord Jesus Christ in Mark 1:35 which states as follows: "Now, in the morning having risen a long while before daylight, he went out and departed to a solitary place, and there he prayed." Practice the act of showing up in the Lord's presence with a grateful heart. Psalms 100:2 states – "Serve the Lord with gladness; come before his presence with singing." Note that the Bible texts states that you should come before the Lord with gladness, not with grumpiness! Also, show up in the Lord's presence with a listening heart. Samuel had a listening heart in I Samuel 3:10, when he said, "Speak, for your servant hears." Have a listening heart as you read the Word and as you walk with God. Pastors, always rest for one hour every day by having unhurried and uninterrupted time with the Lord. Pastors are required to prepare sermons every week, visit people who are in need, and do many other ministry demands, but they must be like Mary who chose the most necessary thing in life that is, sitting at Jesus' feet and listening to His words.

AN ENCOUNTER WITH JESUS

"Come to me, all you who are weary and burdened, and I will give you rest" (Matthew 11:28).

Imagine that Jesus is standing before you now. He's gazing intently at you, His Beloved. Jesus' eyes are full of compassion and as you listen closely, you hear Him say, "Come to me and learn from me and you can find rest."

Ask Jesus to show you ways that He is offering to gently teach you and train you – so that you can find rest.

Wait quietly and listen to the Lord, then offer these prayers.

Jesus, would You show me how to...
I want to learn how to...
I want to join You in journey of life/ministry.
I'm relying on You to carry the load of...

Wait quietly again and the Holy Spirit speak words of comfort, reassurance and guidance. Feel the Savior's presence and relax in His provision.

2. Rest for one day every week. The Biblical word "Sabbath" literally means ceasing. It is a rest from work; it's a break. The main Bible passage for the Sabbatical order is Genesis 2:2-3 And on the seventh day God ended His work which He had done, and He rested on the seventh day from all His work which He had done. Then God blessed the seventh day and sanctified it, because in it He rested from all His work which God had created and made in which God rested from His work. Literally, he ceased from His labor after creating the universe. And, it is applicable to people; His covenant people should rest from time to time. It was not that God was weary in His strength. He is Omnipotent. God created the Sabbath day as His sacred space of rest; He is the king seated upon His throne and asks us, the people under His rule and reign, to observe this same practice. Jesus urges His followers to rest in Mark 6:31 And He said to them, "Come aside by yourselves to a deserted place and

rest a while." For there were many coming and going, and they did not even have time to eat.

More so, the Lord modeled that rest when he calmed the storm in Mark 4:35-41. In Soul Keeping, John Ortberg says, "Spend one day a week, 1/7 of your time doing nothing."

Pastor friend, when do you rest each week? When do you stop checking emails, returning phone calls and making hospital visits? If you will spend 24 hours of rest from ministry to renew your relationship with the Lord, to re-engage your spouse on a date, and to enter the world of your children, you will enjoy incredible spiritual renewal. Pastors' advocates should make sure that their pastor friend plans a Sabbath day every week as this would enable him to keep himself away from the Internet and other ministry duties. He can then spend the time in prayer and meditation; invest in his marriage and parental relationships. That period can also involve recreation and exercise. Make sure that your pastor friend is able to take a walk through the woods; or you could go on a golfing trip together, if that is what is needed.

3. Take a rest one weekend every quarter of the year. Reflect again on Jesus' words to His disciples when He said in Mark 6:31, "Come away by yourselves to a remote place, and rest for a while." Select 2-3 days on your calendar for a quarterly departure to an undisclosed place. Go with your family if it's a vacation. Or, go there to spend time alone on personal Bible study and prayer. You can get away to a bed and breakfast or a private lodge somewhere. Or you can go for a marriage retreat. You might want to consider the Galatians 6:6 Marriage Retreats provided by the Great Commandment Network. These retreats can provide refreshment and renewal specifically for ministry couples.

The Christian Hospitality Network (www.thechn.us) offers up to a 50% discount for a pastor and family (as of the time of this writing – October 2017), including a 2-3 day study retreat to seek the Lord for refreshment and direction. Pastors' advocates are advised to take advantage of the special discounted offer from Christian Hospitality Network and make arrangements for your pastor. During the fall of the year, offer your pastor a gift card of $500.00 and point him to the above website where he can book a short vacation. The pastor and spouse can then get away and enjoy refreshment.

4. Have a one-week rest every year. How do Jesus' words to His disciples apply to your life and family? It means that you should use your official vacation time wisely. The Bible says in 2 Corinthians 6:1, "Do not receive the grace of God in vain." Include a Sunday in your vacation plans. Why is that? If you're not taking off all the week for your vacation, you're going to be thinking about the sermon all of our vacation week. If possible, join two weeks of vacation together. Focus the purpose of your vacation on your relationship with God, your spouse and children. The reality today is that most pastors do not use the vacation time allotted to them by the church.

A word of wisdom that I have learned from many years in the ministry is that you should plan for interruptions of your vacation. You can do this by choosing someone to stand in for you while you are on vacation. You could assign the task to a retired pastor, a director of missions, or an area pastor in whom you trust. Communicate your interruption plans to advocates and church leaders. If someone dies, is hospitalized, or if someone in the congregation needs emergency counseling these people understand that they are to cover for you until you return.

5. Take a one-month rest every five years. This is referred to as a Sabbatical. What is a Sabbatical? It is a time of extended rest for the pastor's spiritual refreshment and renewal. Ideally, it is developed jointly with the pastor and his congregation. How long is a Sabbatical? Typically, a Sabbatical will be at least one month, but not longer than three months. Churches should fully support their pastors by giving them salary and benefits during this time and by providing for some of the expenses. Why should a pastor take a Sabbatical? Well, a Sabbatical will make a pastor more productive because taking an adequate rest helps prepare leaders for the ever-growing demands of spiritual leadership. Pastors' advocates, make sure that you understand what a Sabbatical means so that you can represent and defend the cause of your pastor friend before the church leaders and make sure he is given this opportunity. It is very necessary.

Evidence has shown that leaders that go for a rest usually return from their Sabbaticals with a renewed vision for ministry, and they are better empowered for more effective service. A Sabbatical will extend your current ministry because you will come back to your place of ministry and service feeling refreshed and renewed. You will more likely be able to stay longer.

In a recent blog post on the topic of pastoral Sabbaticals, the president of LifeWay Christian Resources reported that evidence has indicated that pastors returning from Sabbaticals served in their ministry locations much longer than pastors that did not take a Sabbatical. Sabbaticals also add months, maybe years to the pastor's life.

Ministry stress, if not handled wisely, can be hazardous to the pastor's health and to his family relationships. Regular Sabbaticals can help ministry leaders to deal with additional stress that is often inevitable in the pastoral ministry. A Sabbatical will also revitalize a pastor spiritually. To be alone with the Lord remains the most important reason why a pastor should take a Sabbatical. This extended time of fellowship with God will allow a pastor to get a renewed vision on God's unique purpose for his life, ministry and church. Have you ever heard that your cellphone will charge faster in the airplane mode? With the GPS lying dormant and all the other wireless radios within the device rendered temporarily inactive, your phone can take a break from activities such as searching for a cellular signal and then focus solely on recharging. If this is true of your phone, imagine how much more you would accomplish for your overall health and well-being if you simply rest a while?

I would like to ask, as you reflect upon each of these points, which of them do you feel the Lord is calling you to work upon in this new ministry strategy of REST?

One hour every day?
One day every week?
One weekend every quarter?
One week every year?
One month every five years?

Prayerfully reflect on the area to which Jesus is calling you. It's good to step aside from a busy ministry schedule and rest for a while. Andy loves to inspire greater confidence, momentum and encouragement to his pastors friends. He has excellent experience on this subject and he has encouraged me and other pastors to maximize this great opportunity called REST.

I (Andy) have no doubt of the importance of this new ministry strategy of REST for pastors. Going back to Exodus and looking at the story of Moses,

Aaron and Hur, we could see a particular time in the ministry of Moses whose hands became weary. That could be taken as a sign of a need for rest. More importantly, there was stress and strain in what he was doing at that time, even as the battle against Amalekites wouldn't go well with Israel army each time his arms were lowered. Upon realizing this, Aaron and Hur raised his arms up, both overcoming his stress and fulfilling his need for some rest from the strain associated with the lifting of his hands.

So what would it look like for the advocate to encourage a pastor's rest? The first approach is to watch for signs of stress in your pastor. As you start and travel along this journey with your pastor as his advocate, you are in the best position to recognize signs of stress in their life.

As you get to know the pastor's family, children and spouse, they may be able to tell you some of signs that reveal when the pastor is experiencing stress. Watch for those signs as you work together. I recommend that you consistently communicate and encourage dialogue regarding these issues. Open conversations help identify the signs of stress in his life. The best communication style is the informal one since this prevents him from having the feeling that he's being interrogated. Once you see those signs of stress, then it is time to act as his advocate by suggesting the need for a short rest. Michael has mentioned numerous options you can explore in dealing with your pastor's need for a rest. For instance, tell him that, once in while, he should turn off his cell phone and other devices. Sometimes, you might not be able to get in touch with your pastor. He needs it.

A MOMENT OF FELLOWSHIP

"Encourage one another..." (Hebrews 10:25).

Plan to have a conversation with your pastor or advocate. Discuss the signs that each of you display when you're stressed and in need of rest.

You will know that I'm feeling stressed when you see me...or hear me...

If you see that I'm stressed, I want you to bring this to my attention. It would mean a lot to me if you said...

Next, hold one another accountable for how well you are prioritizing times of rest. Encourage one another to put specific dates on the calendar as you discuss these specific questions:

When is your time of rest each day?

When is your time of rest each week?

When is your next date night? Family night?

When is your next time of rest this month? What will that look like? How can I help make this happen?

As an advocate, you can also jump in to help your pastor identify church members that have cabins, lake houses, retreat centers, condos, second homes, or any place where the pastor could go to for his rest. It may be hard for the pastor to make that kind of request from church members, but it would not be hard for you. You could easily ask someone, Will you be willing to share your space with the pastor for a couple of times or a few days a year? Remember, however, that if you use these places, we must leave them how we found them. Quite often the owners will have detailed lists of things that are to be done and how the cabin is to be left before you leave.

When I was a Boy Scout, I was taught to leave the trail better than how we found it. Not only will this practice help the person who gave you their place to stay, but also it will offer you a follow-up visit. It's true that people who have second homes genuinely want people to use them as long as they use such places well.

A second word of warning to pastors' advocate is that they should visit the home before the pastor goes to stay there. Check out the condition of the home and ask neighbors about activities that can be done while the pastor is there. If you know your pastor loves golf, then check out the local golf courses. If the pastor loves to fish, check out the fishing spots. Find a place where these activities are available.

Also, bear in mind the expenses that would be involved while the pastor is on vacation. Michael once delivered a sermon wherein he said, "Instead of buying the pastor a deep freezer which will be placed down in their garage, unused, build memories with the pastor's family." Pastors' advocates should therefore ensure that the pastor's vacation will be a time to build memories, and building memories is not dependent on the amount of money spent on the vacation; but rather, it's more important to spend time together. Get into the world of each member of the family, and if possible, assist them in having a wonderful time on their vacation.

Appendix 3* has guides on adding Sabbaticals to the bylaws of your church. As the pastor's advocate, you may also need to be the one to suggest this initiative. If the pastor asks for a Sabbatical himself, he may or may not be received well. On the other hand, you might be able to build support for the pastor and help him develop an attitude of rest.

Take a look at these websites:

- **www.liftyourpastor.com**
- **www.thepastorsadvocate.com**
- **www.care4pastors.com**

These sites offer numerous tools, programs and opportunities that have been created for pastors. As the pastor's advocate, you need to visit this website and encourage your pastor to take advantage of all the opportunities that have been designed for pastors that would like to go on vacation. Without any controversy, taking a break from ministry schedules will greatly help your pastor to become more effective and productive. Moreover, REST is a vital part of God's Kingdom.

** See Appendix 3 for more information on Sabbaticals*

SAMPLE: REST & SABBATICAL PLANNING SHEETS

	20____	20____	20____	20____	20____
JAN					
FEB					
MAR					
APR					
MAY					
JUN					
JUL					
AUG					
SEP					
OCT					
NOV					
DEC					

This graphic is available for download at: **www.liftyourpastor.com**

SAMPLE: REST & SABBATICAL PLANNING SHEETS

	20____	20____	20____	20____	20____
JAN					
FEB					
MAR					
APR					
MAY					
JUN					
JUL					
AUG					
SEP					
OCT					
NOV					
DEC					

This graphic is available for download at: **www.liftyourpastor.com**

CHAPTER 7: REST

Discussion Questions

When do you rest?

____

____

How do your rest?

____

____

How do you know when to rest?

____

____

How can you find time to:

- Rest one hour per day

  ____

- Rest one day a week

  ____

- Rest one weekend a quarter

  ____

- Rest one week a year

  ____

- Rest one month every five years

  ____

CHAPTER 8

A Pastor's Friend Encourages the Pastor in Relational Health

Proverbs 4:23

"Keep your heart with all diligence, for out of it springs the issues of life."

The above Bible verse was King Solomon's wise advise, for the leader to take care of themselves while carrying out spiritual leadership. You will discover that your relationships required careful cultivation of personal and spiritual growth. WE are going to look into that with use of concentric circles in the diagram below. These circles that depict the life a leader are outlined based on our Lord's Great Commission and Great Commandment.

Our Lord's Great Commission:

Matthew 28:18-20

Then Jesus came and spoke to them, saying, "All authority has been given to Me in heaven and on earth. Go therefore and make disciples of all the nations, baptizing them in the name of the Father and of the Son and of the Holy Spirit, teaching them to observe all things that I have commanded you; and lo, I am with you always, even to the end of the age." Amen.

Our Lord's Great Commandment:

Matthew 22:37-40

Jesus said to him, "'You shall love the Lord your God with all your heart, with all your soul, and with all your mind.' This is the first and great commandment. And the second is like it: 'You shall love your neighbor as yourself.' On these two commandments hang all the Law and the Prophets."

Ministry and influence flow out of a common center – first through the leader's intimate relationship with Jesus, and then closeness with spouse and family. Ministry and mission flow out of these abundant relationships. As a spiritual leader, there are important areas to which only you can give careful attention. Think of these relationships, which require your careful cultivation and spiritual growth, as ever expanding concentric circles. These circles of relational health are based on our Lord's Great Commission and Great Commandment, for Great Commission living is empowered by Great Commandment love.

In this diagram, the center circle is the core of the leader's heart; he is to love the Lord supremely. A leader who experiences the Truth will love the Lord with all his heart, soul, strength and mind. He will do that daily by starting his day in the Lord's presence with a grateful and listening heart. Do you remember that Jesus cleansed a group of ten lepers as recorded in the Bible? After receiving the miracle, only one of them came back, falling at His feet to give glory to God for the miraculous healing? See yourself every day as the leper whom Christ has cleansed with His blood, and give Him thanks.

The next concentric circle is to love your spouse. This literally means loving your near one as yourself. In order to love your spouse, you must first know your spouse. This is why 1 Peter 3:7 encourages husbands to dwell with their wives with understanding. Take time to know your spouse and their relational needs. Go on dates frequently so as to spend time together in conversations. In addition, it is important to respond promptly to your spouse's emotional needs on a daily basis by living out Scriptural principles or Romans 12:15 mourn and rejoice together.

CONCENTRIC CIRCLES OF LEADER CARE

We have written an app for iPhone that allows you to pray the concentric circles each day. Find the app in the Apple Store under *"Take 5 Prayer App"*.

The Concentric Circles graphic is available for download at: **www.liftyourpastor.com**

AN EXPERIENCE WITH SCRIPTURE

"...Husbands must give honor to your wives. Treat your wife with understanding as you live together" (1 Peter 3:7).

If you are married, make plans to have this conversation with your wife. (If not married, have this discussion with a mentor or friend. Ask them to share with you how they see your life's priorities). Set aside at least an hour of uninterrupted time and begin the conversation with these words:

I'm committed to living out 1 Peter 3:7 and give you honor and understanding. I would like to understand how I can show more honor to you and to our marriage. Help me understand more of what it would look like and sound like to give you honor...

I'm also asking the Lord to help me deepen my commitment to His priorities. I first want to love the Lord with all of my heart. After my love for the Lord, I want my priorities to reflect love for my spouse, family, friends, church and the lost – in that order. Could you spend some time telling me how I'm doing with those priorities?

After you've had this conversation with your spouse (or close friend, if unmarried), talk to your pastor/pastor advocate. Make specific plans to address any needed changes.

The third concentric circle is: love your children. Your children are gifts from the Lord; they should be valued as your most important church members. Give them attention so that you enter their worlds by participating in what interests them. Plan your ministry schedules around your children's schedules; take time off to be with them; and always prioritize your relationship with them. As a pastor who has been in ministry for a number of years, I would say it's been quite a difficult thing to balance my ministry schedule with sufficient time with my family life. However, I've made it a priority to always try my best when it comes to attending all activities they are involved in.

The fourth Concentric Circle of Leader Care is love expressed toward a community of faith. This means loving the church, this is expressed out of the depth of the inner three circles. Only a healthy pastor with a healthy marriage and family can effectively serve a local church as their servant leader. Lead your local church just as Jesus did. Seek to raise disciples through spiritual leadership. Lead and feed the local church in such a way that will portray you as a shepherd after God's own heart.

The final circle represents imparting your very life and the Gospel. Apostle Paul modeled this in 1 Thessalonians 2:8 by stating, "We were well pleased to impart to you not only the Gospel of God, but also our own lives." As mission leaders empowered by the love of Christ, we can effectively lead the church to declare and demonstrate the Gospel in communities around us. Only you as a pastor can care for these concentric circles of relationships in your life outlined in the given concentric circles. Other church leaders or members cannot give personal care for these areas of your life. That is why King Solomon's words are so important for every spiritual leader. Watch over your heart with all diligence.

AN ENCOUNTER WITH JESUS

"And we are confident that he hears us whenever we ask for anything that pleases him. And since we know he hears us when we make our requests, we also know that he will give us what we ask for" (1 John 5:14-15 NLT).

Reflect on the concentric circles above and then pray these humble prayers to the Lord.

God, which of these relationships would You like to see me give more attention? How do You see these relationships and the priorities of my life?

After you've heard from the Lord, pray a prayer that you can be confident He will hear and answer. Pray with confidence because you know these prayers are pleasing to Him.

- God, I ask for You to deepen my love for You. I want to love You more. Help me to experience more of Your love, so I can love you in return.
- God, I ask for You to deepen my love for my spouse. Help me to...
- God, I ask You to strengthen my love for my kids, especially in... God, I ask You to deepen my love for the church, I particularly need You to expand my love for...
- and show me how to...
- God, I ask You to refresh my love for people outside the church. Help me to see people with a renewed sense of...

Now, here is a word for all pastors' advocates out there. Encourage your pastor friend to grow in each of these areas. Motivate your pastor to love the Lord, their spouse, their children, the church; and to be a loving witness of Christ in the community. Give them freedom to grow and develop in these areas and also give attention to prayer in each of these areas. Let's hear Andy share his experience on how laypeople can encourage their pastor in relational health.

Pastors' advocates should carefully look at this list of concentric circles. It shows a relational principle that works from inside out: our love for our Lord, love for our spouse, love for our children, love for people in the church, and our love for people outside the church. Look into your own life and make sure that you are living well and are healthy in all your relationships. Spend time each day of your life with the Lord; make sure that your relationship with your spouse is all the Lord intends it to be; let your children know that you are there for them and that they are an important part of your life.

Motivate your pastor to love the Lord, their spouse, their children, the church,; and to be a loving witness of Christ in the community.

Be actively involved in church activities that encourage people grow in their faith in Christ. This is called discipleship. Are you working inside your church to help people to grow in their knowledge of Christ? Are you reaching out to people outside the church through evangelism? In all, just make sure that you are following all the areas of concentric circles. These five circles can become a part of what you and your pastor talk about when you meet to spend some time together. You can talk about one thing that is going on in each of the concentric circles.

By the same token, the pastor can ask his advocate a question about how he is doing in each area of his life. This will not only aid in the mutual conversation, it will also give the pastor new ideas that could enhance his relationship with his children and with his spouse. From my years of experience in working with pastors, I have observed that pastors have a tendency to quickly jump to the outside circle; pastors want desperately to reach the lost world for Christ. They have a tendency to move to the outside circle of evangelism, even at the expense of the inner circles, that is, their wife and children. As pastors' advocates, we might be the only ones that can find out if such tendencies are in their lives. We can ask a few probing question in a conversational way so as to get to the root of a particular matter. For example, I love talking about evangelism, but I may ask, "How are you doing with your spouse?" Recognize the fact that pastors will have a tendency to move to the outside circle first.

In my Take Five Retreat Ministry, we bring pastors together to talk about these five areas of their lives. It is a very simple concept. Each pastor would bring one good idea on what he is doing in each of the concentric circles. Each pastor comes with one idea and goes home with fifteen ideas. All the circles are very crucial, the most important circle is spending time with the Lord and loving the Lord. These concentric circles can be a guiding template that a pastor's advocate can use to encourage his pastor in order to help the leader be the best that the Lord wants him to be in all his relationships.

A MOMENT OF FELLOWSHIP

"Two people are better off than one, for they can help each other succeed" (Ecclesiastes 4:9).

Pray together with your pastor or pastor advocate. Ask God to make any needed changes in the area of priorities. Pray with one another.

Heavenly Father, make any changes in my heart and life that You see are needed. Help me to live out the concentric circle priorities. I specifically ask You to change me by...

Pray for one another.

Heavenly Father, I ask you to help my friend by...

Deepen his love for...

Strengthen the relationship with...

Help me know how to encourage...

CHAPTER 8: RELATIONAL HEALTH

Discussion Questions

What is one good idea you have worked on for each concentric circle:

- Love for the Lord

- Love for your Spouse

- Love for your Children

- Love for your Community of Faith

- Love for people outside your Community of Faith

How is your life going in each circle? *(Use the following pages for your notes.)*

How is your life going in the area of love for the Lord?

PASTOR

ADVOCATE

How is your life going in the area of love for your spouse?

PASTOR

ADVOCATE

How is your life going in the area of love for your children?

PASTOR

ADVOCATE

How is your life going in the area of love for your Church?

PASTOR

ADVOCATE

How is your life going in the area of love for people outside of your Church?

PASTOR

ADVOCATE

Print out more of these questions at: ***www.liftyourpastor.com***
or find more in ***DISCUSSION GUIDE I***

CHAPTER 9

A Pastor's Friend Intercedes and Invites Others to Intercede for the Pastor

I Timothy 2:8
"Therefore I want the men in every place to pray, lifting up holy hands without anger or argument."

In this chapter, we're going to talk about an effective ministry called "30+ 1 men of prayer." This idea was first brought to me by Dr. Ronnie Floyd, the pastor of Cross Church in Arkansas, who has twice been elected president of the Southern Baptist Convention. I Chronicles 11 is one of my favorite chapters in the Bible. It talks about the selection of David's warriors, who strongly supported him in his reign as the king of Israel. David was appointed king by the word of the Lord, and these men were totally loyal to him and supported him in his God-given task.

One noticeable characteristic of these 30+ men was their love for the Lord and their loyalty to King David. For instance, Eleazer in I Chronicles 11:12-14 was with David in a battle against the Philistines; he was assigned to be in a field with David, and the Bible says that they "took their stand in the middle of the plot and defended it, they killed the Philistines, and the Lord gave them a great victory." As a pastor, I'm grateful to God that I have 30+1 men of prayer, who continually love and pray for me; and they are loyal to me each day. Each day of the month, one man will take his stand in prayer of intercession for me, asking that the Lord would grant me great victory in the ministry of the Word of God and my service to others. I am grateful that God has given me this wonderful opportunity. Inarguably, good leaders are supported by great laypeople.

AN ENCOUNTER WITH JESUS

"And David became more and more powerful, because the LORD of Heaven's Armies was with him" (1 Chronicles 11:9 NLT).

"Don't be afraid, for I am with you. Don't be discouraged, for I am your God. I will strengthen you and help you. I will hold you up with my victorious right hand" (Isaiah 41:10 NLT).

David was strengthened by the powerful presence of the Lord. David was victorious because the Lord was with him. Reflect for a moment on this truth. The same Lord, who is Lord of Heaven's Armies and was with David, is with you! Jesus doesn't just support men named David who fight battles around Jerusalem, He is with you! Let the prophet Isaiah remind you of God's promise and presence. Soak in the reassuring words of the Lord. Imagine Jesus is sitting beside you and sharing these words:

- Don't be afraid of conflict in the church, I am with you.
- Don't be discouraged of criticism and scrutiny, for I am your God.
- Don't be afraid when attendance isn't what you had hoped, I am with you.
- Don't be discouraged when things take longer than you wanted, I am your God.
- Don't be afraid of change, I am with you.
- Don't be discouraged when family and ministry are hard, for I am your God.
- I will strengthen you. I will help you. I will hold you up with my victorious right hand.

After you have soaked in the promises of the Lord, give Him thanks. Tell Him about your trust and your gratitude.

Lord of Heaven's Armies, I am grateful for your promise to be with me because...

I am grateful for your promise to help me because...

I am trusting You to...

I am counting on You to...and when we are victorious, I will shout your praises because you are my God!

The 30+1 men of prayer strategy is an effective and proven concept by which lay-leaders and pastors' advocates can strengthen their local church pastor and see God's work accomplished in pushing back the host of darkness and reaching many for Christ. Pastors' advocates are hereby encouraged to make some effort in raising a group of men who can support, love and pray for their pastor. They are in the best position to recruit others... Andy was once a part of my 30+ 1 men of prayer. He is going to share details on how the 30+ 1 men operate.

We have included in this chapter a worksheet that gives instructions on how to set up a 30+1 mighty men of prayer ministry in your church. The instruction sheet is pretty easy to read and implement. Truly, implementing the 30+1 prayer strategy is much more than words on paper. There are at least 30 days in most of the months in a calendar year. Some months have 31 days; February has 28 or 29 days. The concept is that the 30+ 1 coordinator prays and fasts for the pastor on the 31st day of each month, and that would mean he prays about 4 or 5 specific days per year. For the rest of the time, his task involves keeping the group together, providing information on the pastor's areas of needs, and following up on any concerns from the group of 30+1.

It's very important that before a man joins the 30+ 1 group, the coordinator should sit down with him and talk deeply about their walk with the Lord. The concentric circles explained earlier could serve as a great tool for discussion on how the person is working on his love for the Lord, his love for his spouse and his children, and his love for people inside and outside the church. 30+ 1 men need to be working to ensure a pure and spiritually balanced life in all areas of the concentric circles. Do they have to be perfect? Absolutely not. Do they need to be working in all aspects of their life? Yes. 30+ 1 also strongly suggests that each man should fast on the day he prays for his pastor. Fasting is a great way to increase your prayer life. When I fast and I feel hunger pangs, those pangs remind me that I have to pray for my pastor.

There are many books and online articles on fasting that you can read in order to learn the best way you can participate in fasting. We also have a thought inside of 30+1 that there is a "No Questions Asked" policy if a man comes and says, "I need to be taken off of the 30+1 roles." When a man has come to this point in his life where he no longer thinks he can pray and fast for his pastor, we want to make it easy for him to leave the 30+1 roles. It's good for the 30+ 1 ministry to always have 5 or 6 men as replacements waiting to take the place of men who need to be removed from the 30 +1 roles. These men (alternates) can still be assigned a day to fast and pray for the pastor. When you have an opening in the 30+ 1 rotation, a new person can easily move to that day.

Pastors, this 30+ 1 ministry is also dependent on you being active and providing the 30+1 men with prayer requests on a monthly basis. Quite often, this can be done on a calendar or a list of numbers 1-31. Let your 30+ 1 prayer partners know about things that are going on in your life, family, ministry, trips, and several other things that need God's intervention or attention. These 30+ 1 men should be a close group of men to the pastor. In our own case, on a quarterly basis or at least twice a year, we like to have a breakfast with our pastor. Such moments afford us the chance to just go around and talk about the things we have prayed about for the pastor since the last time we met.

AN EXPERIENCE WITH SCRIPTURE

"Where there is no guidance the people fall,

But in abundance of counselors there is victory" (Proverbs 11:14 NASB).

Make plans to pray with your pastor/pastor advocate. Pray together about who should be invited to be a part of your 30+1 ministry. Pray for the Lord's direction and wisdom. Pray that He would reveal an abundance of counselors.

Lord of Heaven, we want Your guidance as we approach the 30+1 ministry. We know that there is victory in the abundance of counselors, so we're asking you to reveal the best prayer warriors from our church and community. We need trusted, followers of Jesus who will lift up our pastor. Speak, Lord. We are listening. Show us who should be a part of this trusted group of counselors?

The 30+1 men should know that the pastor may share some sensitive and confidential things with them. They are advised to keep such information private and confidential. There is no room for gossip in 30+ 1 prayer ministry. These men can't just talk about the pastor's concerns in an open way. Otherwise, they will be exposing the pastor's nakedness. If you look at Genesis 9:22-27, you will know that God takes this very seriously. Pastors' advocates should know too, that because they are generally recognized as close companions with the pastor, they will likely receive more phone calls than they have ever gotten. They become a place where people think they can come to gripe about their pastor, or to spread gossip about the pastor. Such people may even suggest their ideas on how they think the church should work. Be aware!

A MOMENT OF FELLOWSHIP

"This makes for harmony among the members, so that all the members care for each other" (1 Corinthians 12:25).

Pastors and pastor's advocates: There will be an increase in harmony within your congregation, when members demonstrate care for one another. Creating this kind of caring environment begins with you. Therefore, as the two of you meet together and as you meet with the members of 30+1, make vulnerability and care for one another a priority. Make these conversations a part of your private meetings and then as appropriate, share these responses with the 30+1 group as well.

One of my recent celebrations in life, has been...
One of my recent celebrations in ministry has been...
I have been depending upon God for
I have needed support recently in...
I need your continued prayer for...
I am feeling discouraged about...
I am feeling anxious about...
I am feeling grateful for...
I am praising God for...

I'll give you a couple of thoughts on meeting with church members from my own experience. First, whenever these people meet with you, always open the conversation with prayer. Let them pray before they talk about anything that is on their mind. I also use this concept: I try to imagine whose banner we are carrying. Quite often when someone comes to you with a concern about their pastor or their church, the individual may be carrying a very different banner. The use of the word banner goes back to medieval times. When king's men were going off to battle, they would place a banner that had the king's crest on it at the front of the battle. The only crest that we should be carrying is the crest of our Lord Jesus Christ and the plan that He has for our local church. Many times, the internal conflicts or ideas are someone's opinion or some other banner that has nothing to do with the vision of the church. Be very careful in these conversations about what's going on with your pastor and the local church. I will also caution you to be careful on what you agree on; always reach an agreement for a reason. Have a summary statement at the end of your meeting, stating all the things that you agreed upon and things wherein you did not reach a mutual agreement.

Sometimes, there may be tough conversations. In such a situation, get back to the $20,000 question ("Can you tell me more about that?") any time you are not sure what to say. It would help you to keep the other person talking more than you do. Try to get to the root of what they are really talking about. There is a concept of communication called the 5 'whys' which can help you. During the conversation, you can come up with a way to ask 'why' five times. Generally, by the fifth time you will have made it to the root of the problem. If you can guide a conversation through the whys, you may be able to unveil the root of the matter. Now, this is not done by just saying "why?" repeatedly. You need to be more creative than that. Try to develop ways by which you can really find out why you are having the conversation and what the conflict or question may be.

Pastors' advocates, you are about to go on an exciting journey with your pastor, a journey that is very important to the Kingdom of Christ. Be strong and get others to help wherever you can.

30 PLUS 1: OVERVIEW

The **30 PLUS 1 (30+1)** is founded on the biblical principles primarily identified in the following passages.

- I Chronicles 11:10-40
- II Samuel 23:8-38

Also, the practical assimilation of information in two publications authored by Dr. Ronnie W. Floyd.

- "God's Gateway to Supernatural Power"
- "The Power of Prayer and Fasting"

A **30 PLUS 1** man is making a volunteer commitment to intercede on behalf of the Lead Pastor for a minimum of one year. The individual will have established a daily quiet time, which includes consistent **Bible reading and prayer** for at least one year.

Because of the specific nature of the task, **"Mighty Men (MM) of God"** as a guardian (Prayer Warrior) (PW) of the Lead Pastor, the following requirements for a frontline assignment are herein described.

1. Commit to a daily quiet time. (Already an established practice).
2. On your assigned day, pray and fast for the Pastor. (fast is a liquid only fast or doctor guided)
3. Protect the Pastor. (This is specific spiritual warfare (prayer) **on behalf of the Pastor**)
   Pray for **PROTECTION** regarding:

a. Marital Relationship
b. Relationship with his children
c. Relating with other Pastors
d. Relationship with the Lord

While this list may seem short, it is critical to the future development of God's work.

For this ministry to function, some key operational areas must be in place.

1. A coordinator for 30 PLUS 1
2. 31 committed and qualified men
3. Mighty Men (MM in "Reserve")

Operationally, the MM will serve as defined in 30 PLUS 1 operations. The procedure outlined will allow administration of assignments as necessary.

The Reserve MM will become qualified by personal application and fill-in service on behalf of an assignee(s).

It is imperative that every MM be cognizant of the due diligence God desires of him.

30 PLUS 1:OPERATIONAL PROCEDURES

The **30 PLUS 1** is founded on the biblical principles as identified in the "Overview".

30 PLUS 1 men are volunteers committed to the Lead Pastor for spiritual warfare prayer and fasting on his behalf. The guidance for the specific prayer direction will come from the Lead Pastor to the 30 PLUS 1 coordinator, who will prepare and distribute any updated requests to the Mighty Men. This update is recommended to come from the pastor once a month or a quarter.

Assignment of Might Men (MM) is **indefinite**, but with the understanding of the following:

1. The MM (and Reserve) has a specific day of the month to pray and fast.
2. The MM responsibility includes accountability for calling the "next day" MM. **Should your day be the last day of the month — 28, 29, 30 or 31** — you will call the MM of Day 1.
3. Should a MM be unable to cover the assigned day, he will adequately in advance call a "Reserve" MM, therefore, the Reserve calls the next day MM.
4. Should a Reserve MM not be available for a one day "fill-in", the MM should provide adequate advance notice to the coordinator, day 31 or the alternate coordinator, day 30. This will ensure the day will be covered.
5. In the event circumstances require and assignment change, i.e.
   - A job relocation
   - An employment adjustment Family situation
   - Other

   The MM will contact the coordinator ASAP. (To allow for potential delays in getting a qualified "Reserve" MM switched to a specific day, a 90 day notice is requested for MM changes.) The "Reserve" MM is accountable to function similar to a MM, but on a day agreed to with the coordinator. The Reserve will become qualified by personal application and fill-in service for the MM.

6. Also, as an assignment opens, as described above (5), a qualified Reserve MM will have first option to fill the opening.
7. The 30 PLUS 1 Ministry will be coordinated by the person assigned day 31 and the person assigned day 30 will be the alternate and function as the backup to the coordinator.
8. 30 PLUS 1 Coordinator's responsibilities include:
    - Obtaining current (monthly, etc.) prayer request of the Pastor.
    - Distribute timely info to MM's and Reserves.
    - Maintain accurate and active roll of MM's and Reserves.
    - Coordinate necessary fill-in coverage.

Provide ministry status and info men's ministry coordinator.

SAMPLE : 30 + 1 PRAYER PARTNERS TABLE

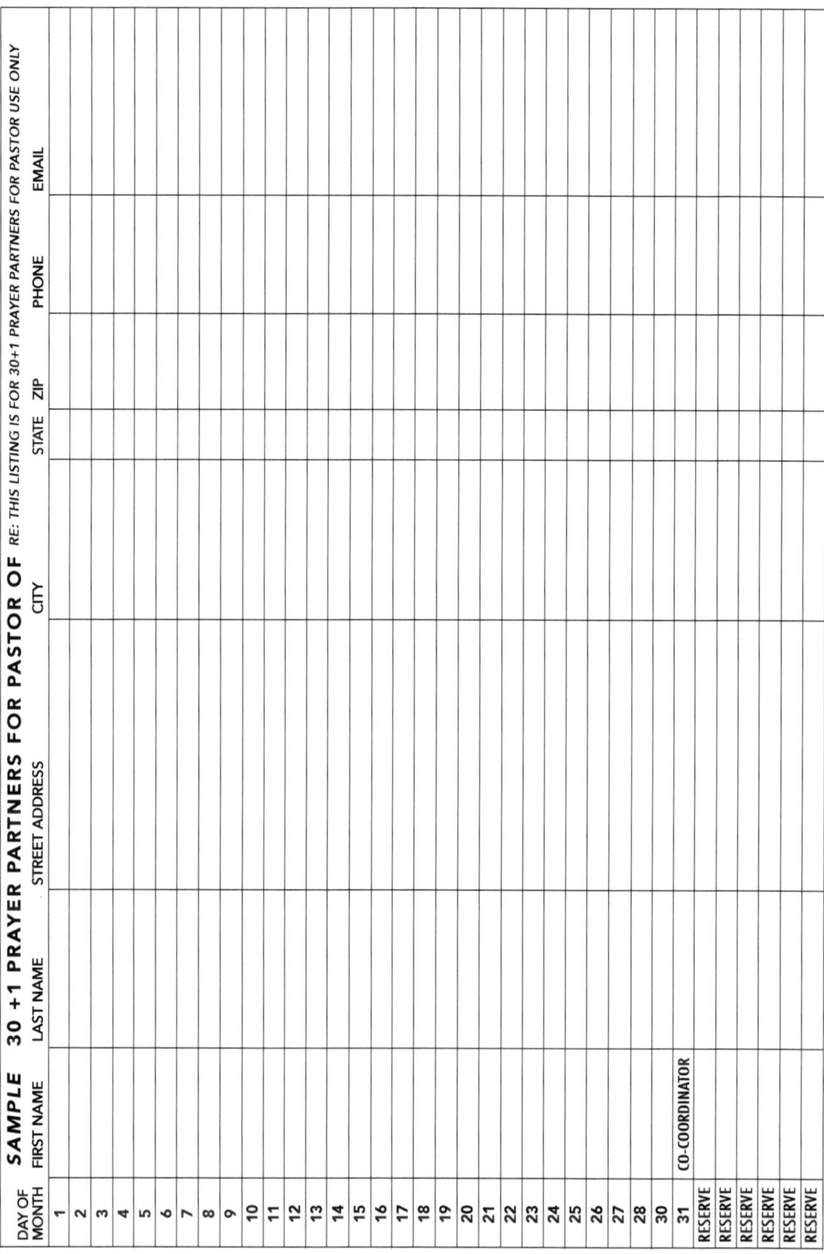

SAMPLE 30 +1 PRAYER PARTNERS FOR PASTOR OF *RE: THIS LISTING IS FOR 30+1 PRAYER PARTNERS FOR PASTOR USE ONLY*

DAY OF MONTH	FIRST NAME	LAST NAME	STREET ADDRESS	CITY	STATE	ZIP	PHONE	EMAIL
1								
2								
3								
4								
5								
6								
7								
8								
9								
10								
11								
12								
13								
14								
15								
16								
17								
18								
19								
20								
21								
22								
23								
24								
25								
26								
27								
28								
30								
31	CO-COORDINATOR							
RESERVE								
RESERVE								
RESERVE								
RESERVE								
RESERVE								
RESERVE								

The Prayer Partners Table is available for download at: **www.liftyourpastor.com**

CHAPTER 9: INTERCEDE FOR PASTOR

Discussion Questions

How can we start a 30 Plus 1 Ministry?

- Who will be our coordinator?

What questions will we want ask potential 30 Plus 1 Men?

What "banners" have you seen Church members carry?

What "banners" have been carried lately?

Have you carried any "banners" that need to be revealed?

CHAPTER 10

A Pastor's Friend is Concerned About the Pastor's Time

Ephesians 5:16
"Making the most of the time, bind up each opportunity because the days are evil." (Amplified Bible)

As I communicate with pastors across North America, one of the recurring concerns that I hear deals with time. How do you balance schedules and find time to do all that you must do? One pastor said, "I love ministry and I am incredibly privileged to do it, but the stress of time takes its toll on me." Another pastor said to me that the unending time-based demands and the expectations of the congregation to be everything to them are overwhelming. Looking at the Bible text above, what does it mean to make the most of the time?

In the Greek text, it means to redeem. The word here is taken from the marketplace. When you go to a supermarket, you'll look for bargains because you know that they will not last long, and that they are quickly changing. Therefore, you'll want to make the most of them and buy them up. This is exactly the word that Apostle Paul used in this text. That is, buy up the opportunities that are being created constantly in these evil days. It's an interesting phrase that says you should buy up each opportunity, that is, you buy time. How can you buy time? How can you buy 60 seconds in a minute? How can you buy 60 minutes in an hour, 24 hours in a day, 7 days in a week, 52 weeks in a year, or 70 years in a lifetime?

As a pastor or as a pastor's advocate, each one of us must understand that it is easy to be caught up in secondary matters or issues that have no eternal value. It is referred to as the "tyranny of the urgent." So here's simple advice for a pastor — spend your time doing things only you can do and let someone else do the rest.

Now, what are some important relationships where you can invest your time? I would like to point your attention to the Concentric Circles of Leader Care. These circles represent relationships of great value in our lives. Look at them again. So how can you redeem time in each of these concentric circles of relationships?

First of all, redeem time by showing your love for the Lord. You can invest your time in your relationship with the Lord. To that effect, Jesus has given His commandment that we should love the Lord with all of our heart, mind, soul, and strength. Recall that Jesus' words to His disciple, Philip, in John 14:8-9, "Lord, show us the Father and it is be sufficient for us;" and Jesus, with a tinge of disappointment, said, "Have I been with you so long, and yet you have not known me?" How long have you known the Lord, dear pastor? Do you really know the Lord? Do you know Him in a deep and abiding relationship?

Love the Lord daily by waiting upon Him to hear His voice; have a devotional walk with Him. Learn to pray Psalms 143:8 on a daily basis, which states, "Cause me to hear your loving kindness in the morning, for in you do I trust. Cause me to know the way in which I should walk, for I lift up my soul to you." Love the Lord by maintaining a spiritually active walk with him. Have a devotional plan, keep a spiritual journal, keep an updated prayer list, don't grow stale in your life, but have a vibrant walk with the Lord! Share what you're learning from the Lord with your wife and children, and even your advocate. In Jeremiah15:16, the prophet of the Lord stated, saying, "Your word was to me the joy and rejoicing of my heart."

AN EXPERIENCE WITH SCRIPTURE

"In my distress I called to the LORD; I cried to my God for help. From his temple he heard my voice; my cry came before him, into his ears" (Psalm 18:6 NIV).

Reflect on your past experiences of "calling out to the Lord," how He heard you and answered your cry. Do you remember times in the past when you found it important to seek the Lord and were glad you did? When have you encountered the challenges of ministry and been blessed because you called upon God? Do you remember crying out to the Lord because you...

- encountered new challenges or obstacles?
- encountered new enemies or attacks?
- faced ministry expansion or redirection?
- were faced with complaints, opposition, or apathy?
- were faced with conflicting demands or priorities?

I remember crying out to the Lord when...

He heard my cry, because...

I am grateful that I went before the Lord because...

Now that you have reaffirmed the benefits of time with the Lord, talk to Him about current needs. Express your faith in how He hears your voice and answers your cry.

Secondly, redeem your time in showing love for your wife. You're the one who can invest time in a marriage relationship with your wife. Jesus said we should love our neighbor as ourselves. Neighbor literally means the closest person to you. Thus, the most important church members you have to serve are your wife and children. To love your near one well requires that you get to know them very well. You must know and accept them for who they are before you can love them as your neighbor.

Over the years, my wife and I have faced many challenges. Liliana is the love of my life, and we have been married for 25 years. I can remember early in our ministry, when we were coming home from a busy day of preaching on a Sunday morning and leadership meetings in the afternoon, I expressed some aggravation toward her. She then responded, saying, "Michael, I wish you would speak to me the way you speak to your church members." That statement became a turning point for me; it was a moment of brokenness for me because I knew that I needed to practice what I was preaching. It dawned on me that the Gospel of grace that I was proclaiming was what I needed in dealing with my wife. Since that day, I have been constantly growing and seeking to redeem valuable time with Liliana.

The third area wherein you need to redeem your time is to love your children. You're the only one who can invest quality time into loving your children. It is alarming to know today that, if care is not taken and we don't enter into the world of our children, a generation of descendants that do not know the Lord may arise (Judges 2:10). So how do you love your children? Always try to enter your child's world. In Philippians 2:5, the Bible exhorts us to have the mind of Christ; it states, "Let this mind be in you that was also in Christ Jesus." What was in His mind? He left heaven and entered into this world, having taken on human flesh. He came as a servant and later died a death at the cross. Our attitude should focus on being like Jesus. Just like Jesus did, we need to enter into our children's world by coming down to their level. We do this by showing interest in their concerns. This is what I often call incarnational parenting. Another way to love your children is simply live life together as Hebrews 12:1 suggests, stating, "Let us run with endurance the race that is set before us." Take the initiative to accept your children as you have been accepted, and to love them as you have been loved. It would add integrity to your faith, even as it produces a deep sense of belonging in the heart of your son or daughter.

Every pastor is advised to place more importance on their children's life and activities than you do for church activities. Place your children's schedule on your calendar because inevitable conflicts may rise as you go on with your ministry tasks; and when they do, talk with your child. If a ministry schedule is pressing, ask your child's permission. Never dismiss a missed opportunity as excusable. I'll never forget the time when our middle daughter Faith, was involved in track events. I had all of her track needs on my calendar except the district track meet, which was not yet scheduled. For some reason, I scheduled an evangelistic outreach to take place on that night in our church.

As I was leading a 100+ people out in evangelism that night, I sensed in my heart that I was about to miss an opportunity with my daughter. I spoke to one of my friends that I wanted to go out visiting with. He then encouraged me that I should go and be with my daughter, promising that everything would be taken care of at our church. I quickly got in my car and drove 15 miles down the road. On getting to the venue of the track event, my daughter was already at the starting line of the race. My eyes met her eyes. I felt she was delighted to see me. That day, she ran the race with all her energy, and it was the best mile that she ever ran in high school. Later she shared with me, that was the best sermon she had ever heard me preach. She is now a daughter who has sensed a call to go to the unreached people groups of the world with the gospel of Jesus Christ. On different occasions, I have attended my daughters' ballet recitals, piano recitals and musical presentations because I loved to enter into their worlds and prove that I care deeply about them.

Furthermore, have a family devotional times where you can share thoughts on Gospel truths from the Bible. One of the practices that we have established in our home during our devotional time is that each one is expected to share three blessings and a prayer request. We have been doing this since our daughters were young. Even though, they are now in a college, we are still doing it with them, and sometimes we do it through Face Time. They share three blessings they have experienced that day and then present a prayer request. Now, that allows us to rejoice for the good things that God is doing in their lives. In addition, we have a practice called a Circle of Prayer. Each family member prays for the person on his or her right.

The fourth area wherein you need to redeem your time is in your love for the church; love expressed toward the household of God, a community of faith people. Again, you're the only one called of God to invest time as the shepherd in leading and loving the local church. John 21:17 states, "Jesus said to Simon Peter the third time, 'Simon son of Jonas, do you love me?' Peter was grieved because He said to him the third time, 'Do you love me?' And he said to him, 'Lord you know all things; you know that I love you.' And, Jesus said to him, 'Feed my sheep.'" A pastor's love for the church and service to others flows out of his deepening love for the Lord. What are some of the ways by which a pastor can love the church? It could be done by serving their interests, based on God's word. You're required to do only what you can do as a pastor and as a leader. What are some of these things that only a pastor can do? Only the pastor can hear from God for the church, prepare a sermon and deliver that sermon. Pastor, focus your time on hearing God and speaking for God. W. A. Criswell stated well a piece of advice I have heeded for years. It goes this way: "Give your mornings to God in study." Stephen Olford said, "Spend time in praying through your sermon until you hear 'Amen' from heaven."

Also, only the pastor can do leadership development. Endeavor to develop leaders in your church staff to love and follow after Jesus. How can you do this as a pastor? It can be done by having regular meetings with leaders and staff, sharing useful thoughts with them in prayer, and modeling before them a deep love for God and a walk in His word. You can also serve the church by having a well-planned and organized calendar of activities and projected ideas. Writing them down and presenting them to church leaders for consideration and implementing is very important for your church. Only a pastor can present a particular vision to the leaders.

Another thing that only pastors can do is ministering to the need of church members, and these include going to those in hospitals to comfort them in such a time of pain and grief, and celebrating with them in life's joyful moments. As a pastor, you're advised to use your afternoons for appointments and visits. The only exceptions would be emergencies. Another matter that only pastors can handle is that of administrative matters. This must be addressed weekly. Otherwise, it will build up on your calendar. For instance, take time to review budgets, write necessary letters, think of stewardship matters, and communicate with the church. As an advocate to your pastor, realize that there are many demands on your friend's life, especially those previously-mentioned areas of important things that can only be done by the pastor. Encourage him, affirm him, and speak words of life to his heart.

The fifth area of your life where you can redeem time deals with getting wholly committed to the Gospel in reaching the community around you. This is what I call "being a loving witness." In John chapter 20:21, Jesus said, "As the Father has sent me, so I send you." The vision that pastors should have is leading every member of the church toward living his or her life as a missionary. Apostle Paul stated in I Thessalonians 2:8, "We were well pleased to impart to you not only the gospel of God but also our own lives." Harness the power of the Gospel of Christ to positively impact on the community around you. Schedule a meeting with community leaders, law enforcement agencies, principals of schools, the mayor of the city, and other established authorities in your community. Make an inquiry about some of needs of the community. Then, seek to lead your church members to meet those needs that are very important to that entire community.

One more tool I've found effective in leading a church on a mission is called the: 3 Circles: Life Conversation Guides (**namb.net**). This is a great way by which you can equip your church to share the Gospel on a regular basis; it will also help you on how you can personally take the lead in sharing the Gospel via conversations with those who are lost. It is very easy to focus on the outer circles of the Concentric Circle of Leader Care, that is, loving the church or being a loving witness of Christ, but you must take time to do what only you can do as the pastor of the church. Let others do the rest.

AN ENCOUNTER WITH JESUS

Teach us to number our days, that we may gain a heart of wisdom" (Psalm 90:12).

Consider some of the challenges that you face with your relationship with Jesus, your spouse, children, the church or evangelism. How do you struggle with the gift of time He has given you? Share those with Jesus now:

Jesus, I am reminded of how I'm struggling with...

It's difficult for me to know how to...

and I need You to teach me how to...

Give me wisdom in how I spend my time, especially how to...

Express your concerns to Jesus and then allow His Spirit to speak words of care and comfort to your heart. Listen for any changes that the Lord wants for your life.

Imagine Christ is talking to you personally. Listen to His voice as He says,

"I want to share in this challenge with you. I am here for you. Give these cares and burdens to Me. I will teach you how to make the best decisions with your time. I will give you wisdom, because I give generously to those who call on Me. You can count on Me because I love you."

As you finish praying, make plans to talk about this prayer experience with your pastor/pastor advocate. Talk about how much it means to have a God who cares about your life, your challenges and your struggles. Share what the Lord revealed to you and any changes that need to be made in your life.

A pastor's advocate can be a strong encourager to a local church pastor on the need to use his time well, that is, you should help him redeem his time. Now, you're about to learn how pastors' advocates can assist their pastors in time management.

As a pastor's advocate, you need to understand that one of our roles may be to guard the pastor's time. This may be done through informal conversations with the pastor about how he is using his time and how he can find new ways to be efficient in his use of time. Make helpful suggestions. Sometimes, you may have to step in to help him address certain issues to free up his time. There have been times where I observed a conversation was getting heated with a church member, and I had to step in to take over the matter. Such cases include aggravations among church members, or among members of staff. More so, it may be something the pastor can't fix at that moment because he needs to focus his attention on something else. In similar cases, as your pastor's advocate, you may have to step in calmly and continue the conversation on his behalf. Now, will this always work? No. Are you the pastor? No. Does that person only want to talk to the pastor? Probably. But then, at that moment, it might not be a productive piece of his time, if he stays back to talk on the matter. It's worthy to note that you must be a humble servant of the Lord to do all these things in the church. Members who recognize you as the pastor's advocate know that you may be the last "in line" to talk to the pastor. Also, be aware that, most of the time, you will be working on your pastor's time and not yours.

As a pastor's advocate, you are there to advocate for the ministry, to increase the ministry, and to help your pastor become more effective in the ministry to which God has called him. In addition, note that a pastor's plans often change. So, be very flexible in handling these changes. For instance, emergencies and funerals may come up at a time he has a ministry schedule he wants to fulfill. Similarly, his plans may change based on the needs of his wife or children. For this reason, a pastor's advocate must not only be willing to change the plans, but he must also remind the pastor that about the important places where he needs to redeem his time. The truth is that all matters are not of the same importance in the life of a pastor.

Of course, Michael has suggested a few things that only a pastor can do. I want to add one more. It is important for the pastor to continually reaffirm the vision for the church. I love working with churches on vision statements. Churches have vision statements that in a lot of ways are very simple to understand and follow. Churches have statements that sound like upward, inward, outward, and some may be worship, grow, or reach. Among other important things that need be done, the pastor is the primary vision caster to the church. You need to state your God-given vision often and more often because you are the steward of that vision. You must make sure that everything done in the church works toward that vision. Use this simple technique I in handling vision statements. Dear pastor, when you feel so sick and tired of talking about your vision that you don't think you can say it another time, it could mean that your best people are just beginning to understand it.

Pastors should note that as they build a godly and friendly relationship with someone as their advocate, they may often need to repeatedly read Proverbs 27:6, "Faithful are the wounds of a friend, but deceitful are the words of an enemy." Several times in this book, we have talked about the place of conversations between pastors and pastors' advocates. Sometimes there might be certain things that pastors may not want to hear from their advocates. Whatever may be the case; these advocates have been put there to have those conversations with them. Don't hesitate to build a relationship that is strong enough to initiate conversations about the pastor's time. There is nothing more precious than the pastor's time. The way your pastor spends the hours in a day, the days in a week, and the weeks in a year matters a lot. Pastors' advocates, help your pastors put the best value to the use of their time.

A MOMENT OF FELLOWSHIP

"Let all that I am praise the LORD; may I never forget the good things he does for me" (Psalm 103:2 NLT).

Close this chapter with a moment of reflection. Allow God to remind you of some of the significant blessings in your life. With all of the pressures of life and ministry, may we never forget the good things that God has done for us. There can be no better use of time than to give praise and honor to the Lord.

Allow God to remind you of a significant blessing in your life.

I remember...

how God recently gave an answer to prayer...

how God met a financial need when ...

how God brought unexplainable peace during a difficult time...

how God brought specific people into my life, just when I needed them...

how God protected me by...

how God guided me and gave me wisdom when...

Pause for a few moments of personal prayer. Tell God about your gratitude. Praise Him for these good things.

God, I am so grateful for the good things that you have brought to my life. I'm especially grateful today for...

I can think of no better way to spend my time than to honor You, so I thank You for...

Finally, share these blessings with your pastor/pastor advocate. Celebrate the goodness of our God together!

CHAPTER 10: PASTOR'S TIME

Discussion Questions

Describe your devotional time

Did you spend quality time with your wife this week?

Did you spend quality time with your children this week?

Are there any "tough conversations" we need to have?

FINAL WORD

A Call to Action for All Pastors

Across the landscape of North America, pastors are going through major problems of discouragement and disillusionment, and they are dropping out of ministry at an alarming rate. This is what we would classify as a downstream problem. Downstream problems can be divided into two classes: plateau declining churches and churches that have closed their doors. Today, we need spiritual churches that will continually flourish in every way, and the only way to have strong, thriving churches is to have strong, effective, and spiritual leaders who can withstand the downstream problems of pastoral needs. Upstream solutions can come from the ministry of a pastor's advocate, and this will result in developing stronger pastors with stronger marriages and families. This in turn will result in the building of a strong, spiritual church that will be able to positively impact the lost with the Gospel of Jesus Christ. Use the Pastor Advocate Covenant on page 185 to help strengthen the Pastor/Advocate relationship.

We hope that God will stir the heart of many more laypeople to become the friend of their pastors. The vision and clarion call that this book is to raise over thousands pastor advocates in North America. This means that pastors will no longer be alone in their local churches. They will have access to an encourager – someone that will be willing to pray for them, and also offer friendly support by standing with them in the task of carrying out the work of the Lord. My friend, Dr. Michael Catt, shares that most pastors resign from leadership capacity in their churches because of three or four people that have become naysayers. A pastor's advocate can stand beside the pastor and support him in good times as well as difficult times that may come to play in the course of ministry. Dear reader, if you're not a pastor, you can choose to become a pastor's advocate for God today.

Our prayer is that God would begin an upstream movement of pastoral advocacy such that every pastor wouldn't be alone as a leader. Every pastor should be greatly supported, encouraged, and strengthened so that God's kingdom can expand and the church will be edified. How can we recruit thousands of pastors' advocates? We can start with just one person.

Pastor, having read this book, you now have an understanding of the concept of having a pastor's advocate. Have you thought of someone in your congregation that might be able to serve the Lord as a good and reliable advocate? Let us know. Dear layperson, it's good that you have read this book. Maybe it was given to you by your pastor. Are you ready to become a pastor's advocate? Let us know. You can simply email us at: **pastor@liftyourpastor.com** or **advocate@thepastorsadvocate.com**. Send an email message to us and you will start receiving helpful information on how to be the best pastor's advocate that you can be.

Use the guide on page 186 to help find your advocate. This communication will come in the form of quarterly newsletter, quarterly suggestions, and quarterly ideas that can enhance your pastor's advocate ministry. Raising thousands of pastors' advocates for pastors will be of great benefit to God's cause. What a LIFT that would bring to a local church pastor! It's going to bring about spiritual growth to God's church. We thank you for reading this book and we hope that you will join us in this ministry.

Yours in good faith,

Andy and Michael

For more information on receiving additional copies (print or PDF) of Lift Your Pastor – Becoming a Pastor's Advocate, go to ***www.liftyourpastor.com*** *and click on "**Book**"*

FINAL WORD: CALL TO ACTION

Discussion Questions

Will you ask a man to be your advocate?

Will you commit to going through this book with him?

DISCUSSION GUIDE I

Chapter Discussion Questions

Print out more of our worksheets at: ***www.liftyourpastor.com***

INTRODUCTION

Discussion Questions

PASTOR

Have you had an advocate in the past?

Have you had times when you needed an advocate?

Do you have someone in mind for a advocate currently?

ADVOCATE

Have you had an advocate relationship with a Pastor in the past?

Have you had an advocate relationship in other areas of your life?

CHAPTER 1: LIFT LOAD OF MINISTRY

Discussion Questions

Describe your average:

- Day ______
- Week ______

What tasks are most draining (burdensome)?

______

How can we work together to lift the load of ministry?

______

How do you pray?

______

- Daily ______
- Weekly ______

PASTOR

Has there been a time in your ministry when you faced trials?

______

Has there been a time in your ministry when you felt alone and needed an advocate?

______

ADVOCATE

How do you personally serve your Church?

______

How do you personally support your Pastor?

______

Have you ever been attacked for your support of your Pastor?

______

- How? ______
- What did you do to handle it?

  ______

CHAPTER 2: REMOVE ALONENESS

Discussion Questions

BOTH

Have you ever stumbled in your ministry? ______________________

Have you ever felt overworked in your ministry? ______________________

Have you ever had a friend to aid you in ministry? ______________________

Have you ever taken a "call" to help your Pastor? ______________________

Have you ever had a true accountability partner?

____

Do you recognize and know each other's family?

____

Do you have each other's contact information? ______________________

What does the caller ID say when each calls the other?

____

Do you have a "Kathy's Kitchen" type of place?

____

Does "pride" get in your way? ______________________

- What does "pride" look like for you?

  ____

What does it look like when you are overworked?

____

- Physically?

  ____

- Emotionally?

  ____

CHAPTER 3: ENCOURAGER

Discussion Questions

PASTOR

Have you faced opposition in your ministry?

From outside?

From inside?

Have you ever felt insecure about your ministry?

ADVOCATE

Do you encourage those around you?

Are you more apt to listen than talk?

Do you use open ended questions often in conversation?

Can you tell me more about that?

What are major stress points in your week?

How do you like to be encouraged?

What makes you feel insecure?

What can you do to be a better listener?

CHAPTER 4: CALL TO MINISTRY

Discussion Questions

PASTOR

Describe your call to ministry

Describe your sermon prep

Daily

Hour commitment

BOTH

What are your skills?

Passions?

How can they be used together?

What are your top 3 spiritual gifts?

RESOURCE LINK (SPIRITUAL GIFTS INVENTORY FROM LIFEWAY):
http://www.lifeway.com/lwc/files/lwcF_MYCS_030526_Spiritual_Gifts_Survey.pdf

CHAPTER 5: TRANSPARENCY

Discussion Questions

What are you transparent about?

What do you need to be more transparent about?

Are there any confessions you need to make today?

Do you have a "quiet place" to study?

How can you protect that place?

How and what can I (should I) hold you accountable for?

CHAPTER 6: PRAYER

Discussion Questions

Do you pray daily for your Church?

Do you pray daily for your advocate?

Do you pray daily for your Pastor?

PASTOR PRAYER REQUESTS

ADVOCATE PRAYER REQUESTS

PASTOR PRAYER REQUESTS

ADVOCATE PRAYER REQUESTS

PASTOR PRAYER REQUESTS

ADVOCATE PRAYER REQUESTS

CHAPTER 7: REST

Discussion Questions

When do you rest?

How do your rest?

How do you know when to rest?

How can you find time to:

- Rest one hour per day
- Rest one day a week
- Rest one weekend a quarter
- Rest one week a year
- Rest one month every five years

CHAPTER 8: RELATIONAL HEALTH

Discussion Questions

What is one good idea you have worked on for each concentric circle:

- Love for the Lord

____

____

- Love for your Spouse

____

____

- Love for your Children

____

____

- Love for your Community of Faith

____

____

- Love for people outside your Community of Faith

____

____

How is your life going in each circle? *(Use the following pages for your notes.)*

CONCENTRIC CIRCLES OF LEADER CARE

We have written an app for iPhone that allows you to pray the concentric circles each day. Find the app in the Apple Store under *"Take 5 Prayer App"*.

The Concentric Circles graphic is available for download at: **www.liftyourpastor.com**

How is your life going in the area of love for the Lord?

PASTOR

ADVOCATE

How is your life going in the area of love for your spouse?

PASTOR

ADVOCATE

How is your life going in the area of love for your children?

PASTOR

ADVOCATE

How is your life going in the area of love for your Church?

PASTOR

ADVOCATE

How is your life going in the area of love for people outside of your Church?

PASTOR

ADVOCATE

How is your life going in the area of love for the Lord?

PASTOR

ADVOCATE

How is your life going in the area of love for your spouse?

PASTOR

ADVOCATE

How is your life going in the area of love for your children?

PASTOR

ADVOCATE

How is your life going in the area of love for your Church?

PASTOR

ADVOCATE

How is your life going in the area of love for people outside of your Church?

PASTOR

ADVOCATE

How is your life going in the area of love for the Lord?

PASTOR

ADVOCATE

How is your life going in the area of love for your spouse?

PASTOR

ADVOCATE

How is your life going in the area of love for your children?

PASTOR

ADVOCATE

How is your life going in the area of love for your Church?

PASTOR

ADVOCATE

How is your life going in the area of love for people outside of your Church?

PASTOR

ADVOCATE

CHAPTER 9: INTERCEDE FOR PASTOR

Discussion Questions

How can we start a 30 Plus 1 Ministry?

- Who will be our coordinator?

What questions will we want ask potential 30 Plus 1 Men?

What "banners" have you seen Church members carry?

What "banners" have been carried lately?

Have you carried any "banners" that need to be revealed?

CHAPTER 10: PASTOR'S TIME

Discussion Questions

Describe your devotional time

Did you spend quality time with your wife this week?

Did you spend quality time with your children this week?

Are there any "tough conversations" we need to have?

FINAL WORD: CALL TO ACTION

Discussion Questions

Will you ask a man to be your advocate?

Will you commit to going through this book with him?

EXPERIENCING SCRIPTURES REVISITED

Complete Collection

AN ENCOUNTER WITH JESUS

Therefore, there is no condemnation for those who are in Christ Jesus. (Romans 8:1).

Who will bring any charge against those whom God has chosen? It is God who justifies. Who is he that condemns? Christ Jesus, who died – more than that, who was raised to life – is at the right hand of God and is also interceding for us. (Romans 8:33-34).

Pastor/Leader:

Do you sometimes feel accused? Have you experienced the rejection or criticism of others? Do you feel others are often judging you or evaluating you?

Or do you, at times, feel that you deserve to be condemned? Is there an area of your life that has gone unconfessed or that repeatedly causes you to struggle?

Are you burdened by the struggles of this world? Are you weary because of the stress of this life? Are you tired of problems or discouraged by affliction?

To everyone who experiences these feelings of accusation or criticism, the Apostle Paul poses the question: "Who will bring any charge against you?" (Romans 8:33). Paul goes on to answer this question with a declaration of truth. He reminds us that there is only One person with the right and power to accuse, criticize, or condemn: "It is God who justifies" (v. 33). Knowing that we might resist such a liberating truth, Paul asks again, "Who is he that condemns?" (v. 34). Again, we read Paul's reminder that there is only One who has the right to condemn us. Only Jesus has the right to and power to judge, but notice what He is doing for those who believe: He is praying for us (v. 34)! The One person who has the right to judge us – is the same One who is interceding on our behalf! This is why the apostle can say, "There is now no condemnation" for us (v. 1). The One who can condemn us is praying for us.

Allow the Holy Spirit to lead you into a personal experience of Romans 8:33-34 as you encounter Jesus.

Close your eyes and imagine the scene of a courtroom. The words Paul uses are legal terms – words that we hear in courtrooms today: "bring charge" and "condemn." Feel the intimidation of your surroundings. Feel the stress and pressure of the legal environment.

Now, using your imagination look around and see the faces of the people who are in the courtroom with you. Imagine that the faces you see in the jury are the people who have been harsh, cruel, critical or judgmental. The people you see staring back at you are the same ones who have neglected you, abandoned you, betrayed and hurt you.

But remember the truth: Only Jesus Christ, the Righteous One has the right to judge and the power to condemn.

As you sit in the courtroom, your attention turns as you hear heavy wooden doors open. Jesus enters the room. You see His flowing robes, sandaled feet and bearded face. And rather than take His place behind the judge's bench, Jesus stands beside you. He slowly eases His arm around your shoulder and gently leads you to join Him. The two of you kneel together in prayer.

You don't notice it at first, but as you pause to listen, you hear Jesus praying. He is praying about the things on your prayer list. He's praying for the needs in your life and the concerns of your heart. Then you hear Him ask, "Where are your accusers?" You raise your head and realize that the courtroom is empty. Everyone one of those faces that were filled with condemnation and judgment are now gone. Each person who brought a charge against you has vanished. Everyone who responded with neglect or abandonment has disappeared. Jesus then proclaims, "Neither do I accuse you."

The only One who can condemn you, prays for you! The only One who is equipped to judge you, doesn't. The Holy One of the Universe prays for you!

Pause now and allow the Holy Spirit to fill your heart with wonder and gratefulness to Jesus. Spend the next few moments allowing Him to plant these truths into your heart and then share your words of thanks:

Thank you, Jesus for your incomparable love. I praise you because of your grace. I'm filled with gratitude because you pray for me, rather than condemn me. I'm thankful that you pray for me, instead of judge me. Lord, I'm especially grateful to you because...

AN EXPERIENCE OF SCRIPTURE

"God, who comforts the downcast, comforted us by the coming of Titus" (2 Corinthians 7:5).

Reflect on this passage for a moment. Here are some of the truths that are captured in this short verse of the Corinthians:

The God of the universe, full of power and strength, apparently chose to use another person to extend His comfort to a weary, spiritual leader. Titus was a trusted follower of Jesus because it had been Titus who was with Paul in his second imprisonment in Rome. Can you imagine the bonding experiences they must have shared in a Roman jail? Titus had also been sent to establish the church at Crete, therefore Titus and Paul shared many things in common: history, struggles, ministry, and their unquenchable faith.

Reflect for a few moments on the unique relationship that must have existed between Paul and Titus.

Now celebrate the blessing of the pastor/advocate relationship and prepare to share your celebrations.

Reflect on a time when God brought a "Titus" into your life to encourage you, comfort you and support you during a time of distress.

I remember a time when God brought ________ into my life. I'm especially grateful for this time and for this person because...

A MOMENT OF FELLOWSHIP

"And you are the body of Christ and members individually" (1 Corinthians 12:27).

Reflect on one of your own experiences of interdependence. Then complete the following sentences:

I recall a time when I needed ________ (specify a person's name) and their __________ (gifts, talents, expertise, advice, counsel, comfort, wisdom or life experience).

The Lord used their (gifts, talents, expertise, etc.) in my life to give _________ (encouragement, comfort, affirmation, etc.) to me.

Share your responses with your pastor or pastor advocate and then together, prayerfully claim the promises of 1 Corinthians 12:25: "That there should be no division in the body, but the members should have the same care for one another."

A MOMENT OF FELLOWSHIP

"Don't be so naive and self-confident. You're not exempt. You could fall flat on your face as easily as anyone else. Forget about self-confidence; it's useless. Cultivate God-confidence" (1 Corinthians 10:12 MSG).

Reflect on the times when you may have been naïve or self-confident, only to fall flat on your face. Then consider how circumstances might have been different if you had been able to fall into the arms of a trusted friend. Prepare to talk about this difference with your pastor or advocate.

My naïve perspective or self-confidence got me into trouble when...

Things would've have been much different if ...

In the future, if you see my naïve perspective or over-confidence in the future, I give you permission to call it to my attention. I will receive that feedback from you best as you...

(For example: talk to me privately, reassure me that you care about me first, tell it to me straight and then offer support, etc.)

AN ENCOUNTER WITH JESUS

"But I will send you the Advocate—the Spirit of truth" (John 15:26 NLT).

Every pastor and every church leader can benefit from more encounters with our Advocate – Holy Spirit. The Gospel of John reminds us that the Spirit of truth is with us and actually within us. Pause for moment and consider: The Father loved you so much that He didn't want to leave you without an Advocate. Jesus knew that you would face many of life's struggles and winter seasons of life. Because of His heart for you, Christ sent the Spirit to be your Guide and your Comforter. Jesus couldn't bear the thought of leaving you alone, so He provided an Advocate – One who is always with you because He lives in you!

Prayerfully consider the amazing truth that God cared so much about your aloneness, that He provided an Advocate. Allow the Holy Spirit to speak to you and confirm His presence. Hear His voice of affirmation, encouragement, comfort and support. What does it do to your heart to reflect on these truths?

When I consider that Christ cared about me so much that He provided an Advocate who is always with me and always caring for me, I feel...

My heart is moved with gratitude because...

AN EXPERIENCE WITH SCRIPTURE

"God opposes the proud but gives grace to the humble" (James 4:6 NLT).

One of the best ways to demonstrate humility is to vulnerably admit your need. Prepare for a conversation with your pastor or advocate. Share your responses to the following, demonstrating your humility and allowing the Lord the opportunity to bless your relationship with grace.

You'll know that I need "a call" when ...

(For example: I'm overwhelmed with ministry activities; the kids and my wife are starting school – that's an especially busy time of year, I get short-tempered or critical, etc.)

It's at those times when I need to sense that I'm not alone. I would feel less alone if we could...

(For example: I would feel less alone if we could get together for breakfast once a week; pray together before worship services, plan some fun things to do together as families, etc.)

AN ENCOUNTER WITH JESUS

Pause for a few moments and ask the Lord to help you encounter His love in fresh, new ways. The passage above reminds us of the character of God. God comforted the Apostle Paul when his body was weary and when trouble was on every side. God felt compassion when Paul was afraid and when he was surrounded by conflict and turmoil. Reflect on the truth of this passage and what it says about God's response to our struggles. Hebrews 13:8 tells us that Jesus is the "same yesterday, and today and forever." So the same God who felt compassion for the Apostle Paul feels compassion when he sees your weariness. The same God, who comforted Paul when he was afraid and downcast, is the same God wants to comfort you.

First, tell God about any circumstances that are troubling your heart. Pour out your heart before the Lord.

God, at times I am weary of ...

I need you to know that I feel so afraid when ...

God, when I see the conflict around __________, I feel...

I need your help because it seems like there are troubles on every side because...

Now, make the truths of 2 Corinthians 7:5-7 more personal. Imagine that Jesus is standing beside you. His face is full of kindness and understanding. He puts his hand on your shoulder and begins to speak.

"Thank you for pouring out your heart to Me. Just as I comforted my brother, Paul, I want to do the same for you. I know you are weary and often tired. It hurts my heart to see you struggle. I see the times when you are afraid. It's at those times, when I whisper a prayer to the Father, asking Him to give you peace. I too, see the conflict that surrounds you and I feel great compassion. My heart aches when the people I love aren't experiencing unity and love. I hurt with you because of the trouble.

I see the struggles and want you to know that you are not alone. I am the same One who comforted Paul and I long to give that same compassion for you, My Beloved."

Receive these words. Let the God of all comfort, comfort you in this very moment.

Now, pause to give Him thanks.

God, thank you for your compassion. Thank you for loving me and comforting me in my struggles. I'm especially grateful for your compassion because...

AN EXPERIENCE WITH SCRIPTURE

"Freely you have received, therefore freely give" (Matthew 10:8)

Reflect on the fresh experience of comfort that you have just shared with Jesus. Recall the other times when you have received compassion and care from the Lord. You have freely received comfort from the God. Now, how might you freely give? Ask God to speak:

Pastor: God, you've freely given comfort to me. Who needs some of that same compassion delivered through me?

Pastor Advocate: "God, you've freely given comfort to me. How can I share Your compassion with my pastor? Show me how to comfort in weariness, trouble, conflict or fear. Speak Lord, I want to hear you."

A MOMENT OF FELLOWSHIP

"...So that through perseverance and the encouragement of the Scriptures we might have hope" (Romans 15:4).

Plan a conversation with your pastor or pastor advocate. Begin your conversation with these words and then listen carefully to one another.

At times, I need God's strength to persevere in...

The Scripture, 2 Corinthians 7:5-7 gives me encouragement because...

God's heart of compassion gives me hope because...

At any time in this conversation, look for opportunities to deepen your understanding of your pastor/pastor advocate by asking:

Can you tell me more about that?

AN EXPERIENCE WITH SCRIPTURE

"We have placed our confidence in him, and he will continue to rescue us. And you are helping us by praying for us" (2 Corinthians 1:10-11).

Pastor: As you think about these roles of ministry (lead, guard and oversee), which of these might God want to strengthen in you? Ask your advocate, spouse or trusted friend to help you by praying for you.

Share your responses to these sentences and then ask for prayer.

I think God would want to strengthen my leadership by...

I think God might want to strengthen the way I guard our congregation by...

I think God would want to strengthen the way I oversee our church by...

Now, would you pray for me and help me by your prayers?

Pastor Advocate: As you think about these ministry roles (lead, guard, oversee), which of these might God want to strengthen in you – as you relate to your family, ministry leaders, or co-workers? Ask your pastor, spouse or trusted friend to help you by praying for you.

Share your responses to these sentences and then ask for prayer.

I think God would want to strengthen my leadership by...

I think God might want to strengthen the way I guard...

I think God would want to strengthen the way I oversee...

Now, would you pray for me and help me by your prayers?

A MOMENT OF FELLOWSHIP

"So then, just as you received Christ Jesus as Lord, continue to live in him" (Colossians 2:6 NASB).

Reflect on your encounter with Jesus above. In what ways did you yield to the leading of Jesus? In what areas, did you sense a need to learn from him? Talk about these insights with your pastor/pastor advocate.

I need to learn more about leading/guarding/overseeing from Jesus, especially in the area of...

I sense that He wants me to become more ___________ (bold, courageous, loving, gentle, forgiving, accepting, discerning, etc.) I know that I'll only learn this from Him.

AN ENCOUNTER WITH JESUS

"Take my yoke upon you and learn of me, for I am gentle and humble" (Matthew 11:29).

Imagine Christ standing before you. His eyes are kind and gentle. His expression is loving and welcoming. As you look more closely, you notice that Christ is wearing a yoke – a yoke of service and love. The purpose of this yoke is to allow the One who is experienced to train another. Jesus stands before you wearing the yoke, and the other side of the yoke is empty. You realize that Jesus is inviting you to join him in loving, leading and serving others well. He is the master teacher and the humble servant who can train, equip, and guide you. Listen to His words:

"Take my yoke upon you and learn from me. I am a gentle and humble teacher who can help you as you lead, guard and oversee the ones whom I have entrusted into your care. Come and take the other side of the yoke and together, we can love your near ones well! Come to me and learn what I know about the people you lead. Learn from me how to guard and protect. Learn from me how to guide and oversee the precious people around you.

Pause in prayer. Tell Jesus about your willingness to join Him in the yoke and learn from him.

Lord Jesus, I do want to join you in better loving and leading...

I yield myself to you. I do want to learn from you, especially how to...

Thank you for sharing this burden and showing me how to...

AN ENCOUNTER WITH JESUS

"For the LORD... takes the upright into his confidence" (Proverbs 3:32 NIV).

Reflect on the times when you have sensed that the Lord has taken you into His confidence? When has he shared special insights with you? When have you heard from the Lord during your times of prayer, study or reading of Scriptures? When has God revealed himself or his plans through another believer or moment of worship?

I remember having a personal encounter with Jesus, when he took me into his confidence and...

- drew me close to him by...
- gave me specific direction about...
- provided a warning about...
- revealed more of himself as...
- confirmed that...
- affirmed me for...
- reassured me that...

Ask the Holy Spirit to help you remember the times when the Lord has revealed himself to you in these ways. Allow God to renew your confidence. Remember that it is the God of all creation who has taken you into his confidence. Let him confirm your calling and purpose, then thank him in prayer. Let your confidence come from God.

God, thank you for revealing yourself to me. I stand sufficient and confident in your calling because of who you are and what you have done.

AN EXPERIENCE WITH SCRIPTURE

"Search me, O God, and know my heart; test me and know my anxious thoughts. See if there is any offensive way in me, and lead me in the way everlasting" (Psalm 139:23-24 NASB).

Be still before the Lord and make the same request of Psalm 139. Ask God to search your heart and identify any parts of your life that need to be changed in order to see more and more Christ-likeness. Your prayers might begin like these:

Search me, O God, and show me the sins that hinder me from becoming more like you. Free me from anything that's immoral or evil. Free me from any malice, deceit, hypocrisy, envy or slander. I want to have a clean mind and heart, so show me anything about my life that needs to change.

Search me, O God, for unresolved emotions. Free me from any guilt or condemnation, any anger or bitterness, any fear or anxiety. Free me to live each moment "in the present" with you. What parts of my emotions need to change?

Search me, O God, for any childish things that distract me from becoming more like you. Free me from rationalizing my behavior and blaming others. Free me from idle chatter and self-focus. Help me to practice personal responsibility before you and others. What are the childish things that need to be put away?

Search me, O God, for areas of self-reliance that prevent me from becoming more Christ-like. Free me from my thoughts, my ways, my ideas and my goals. I want to embrace Your thoughts,

Your ways, Your ideas and Your goals. Show me any ways that I am putting my plans above Yours.

Pause and wait for the Lord to speak to you about one or more of these areas. Then yield to him, even though you may not know all that will be necessary for change and Christ-likeness. Pray a prayer of yieldedness.

Lord, I sense the need to put away __________ from my life. Even though I don't know all that this change will require, I yield to You. Remove this from my life so that I can become more and more like You.

A MOMENT OF FELLOWSHIP

"Because we loved you so much, we were delighted to share with you not only the gospel of God but our lives as well" (1 Thessalonians 2:8).

Plan a time with your pastor/pastor advocate and share your responses to the following. Let this be a time of sharing the story of your lives together.

I've had these conversations with Jesus lately...

I've heard the Lord say...

As I reflect on my relationship with my spouse (or closest friends if not married), and I feel...

When I think about my relationship with my kids (if applicable), I feel ______ because...

My greatest celebration within ministry right now is...

My greatest challenge in ministry right now is...

AN EXPERIENCE WITH SCRIPTURE

"Pray for us. Pray that the Lord's message will spread rapidly and be honored wherever it goes..." (II Thessalonians 3:1 NLT).

Pause now and do the Book, take the time to actually be a "doer" of the Word. If you are a pastor's advocate, pause and pray for your pastor right now. If you are a pastor, take this time to pray for one of your fellow ministers. Pray for another pastor's life and ministry.

Pray for the concerns of the pastor's heart and ministry. If you don't know specifics, ask the Lord for wisdom in what to pray. Then, pray that God's message, delivered through your pastor, will spread rapidly and will be honored among believers and lived out with passion.

God, I want to pray for ______.

Please strengthen my friend's personal/family life by...

Strengthen my friend's ministry by...

I ask You to give my pastor boldness to preach Your message and that this message would spread rapidly among our congregation and community. Help us live out Your truth, so that we bring honor to You.

A MOMENT OF FELLOWSHIP

"...I urge you in the name of our Lord Jesus Christ to join in my struggle by praying to God for me. Do this because of your love for me, given to you by the Holy Spirit" (Romans 15:30 NLT).

As the pastor's advocate, reflect on a few church leaders who might join you in the calling of praying for your pastor. Ask these individuals to be a part of a team of leaders who lift up your pastor in prayer.

Pastor, ask yourself: "Who would I like to join me in the struggles of ministry? Who should be a part of the team that prays for me?" Ask these individuals to be a part of a team who lifts you up in prayer.

Ask the Lord for wisdom and then write the names He gives you here:

Along with this prayer team, make specific plans for prayer: before services, at holiday seasons, during conflict, for a pastor's marriage and family, at a specific time of day or week.

AN ENCOUNTER WITH JESUS

"He always lives to intercede for them" (Hebrews 7:25).

There were many times when the disciples watched Jesus move to a private place and pray. Christ modeled the importance of prayer. Prayer was the lifeline of the Savior while he was here on earth. Prayer connected the Father with the Son.

If we know that prayer is so important, why do we often struggle to pray? Could it be that we've missed a relational connection of prayer? Spend the next few moments asking the Lord for a renewed perspective on prayer.

The writer of Hebrews tells us that Jesus is still modeling the importance of prayer. In fact, Scripture reminds us that he lives to intercede for us. Pause and reflect for a few moments on the personal truth of this passage. You have a Savior who is praying for you!

Imagine a scene that's similar to the story in the Garden of Gethsemane. Jesus comes to the garden with his disciples. He asks them to wait while he kneels nearby in prayer. Imagine that, on this day, you are one of those disciples. After some time, you leave the others and walk toward the place where Jesus is praying.

You hear him talking to the Father, but can't quite make out what he is saying. As you quietly approach, you hear Jesus praying...and he is praying for the needs of your life. He is interceding for the concerns of your heart and pleading to the Father on your behalf. Jesus is praying for you!

What does it do to your heart to know that Jesus, your Savior and your Lord, loves you so much that he is interceding for you? Tell him now:

Jesus, when I consider that you are praying for me – for the needs of my life and the concerns of my heart – I feel...

Now that you have a fresh view of our Savior and how he intercedes for you, how might that impact your desire to pray? Talk to Jesus about your renewed desire to join him in prayer.

Jesus, I am reminded of how you are always praying for me, interceding for me and talking to the Father on my behalf, and that makes me want to...

AN EXPERIENCE WITH SCRIPTURE

"Come away by yourselves to a remote place and rest for a while" (Mark 6:31).

Spend an hour alone with the Lord. This isn't the time for Bible study or sermon preparation. This is just a time for you to go away to a remote place and be with Jesus. After you have quieted your heart, ask the Savior to reveal areas of life where He longs to give you rest.

Jesus, I know that I am weary of...

I am burdened because...

In what ways do you want to give me rest? Speak Lord, I'm listening...

AN ENCOUNTER WITH JESUS

"Come to me, all you who are weary and burdened, and I will give you rest" (Matthew 11:28).

Imagine that Jesus is standing before you now. He's gazing intently at you, His Beloved. Jesus' eyes are full of compassion and as you listen closely, you hear Him say, "Come to me and learn from me and you can find rest."

Ask Jesus to show you ways that He is offering to gently teach you and train you – so that you can find rest.

Wait quietly and listen to the Lord, then offer these prayers.

Jesus, would You show me how to...

I want to learn how to...

I want to join You in journey of life/ministry.

I'm relying on You to carry the load of...

Wait quietly again and the Holy Spirit speak words of comfort, reassurance and guidance. Feel the Savior's presence and relax in His provision.

A MOMENT OF FELLOWSHIP

"Encourage one another..." (Hebrews 10:25).

Plan to have a conversation with your pastor or advocate. Discuss the signs that each of you display when you're stressed and in need of rest.

You will know that I'm feeling stressed when you see me...or hear me...

If you see that I'm stressed, I want you to bring this to my attention. It would mean a lot to me if you said...

Next, hold one another accountable for how well you are prioritizing times of rest. Encourage one another to put specific dates on the calendar as you discuss these specific questions:

When is your time of rest each day?

When is your time of rest each week?

When is your next date night? Family night?

When is your next time of rest this month? What will that look like? How can I help make this happen?

AN EXPERIENCE WITH SCRIPTURE

"...Husbands must give honor to your wives. Treat your wife with understanding as you live together" (1 Peter 3:7).

If you are married, make plans to have this conversation with your wife. (If not married, have this discussion with a mentor or friend. Ask them to share with you how they see your life's priorities). Set aside at least an hour of uninterrupted time and begin the conversation with these words:

I'm committed to living out 1 Peter 3:7 and give you honor and understanding. I would like to understand how I can show more honor to you and to our marriage. Help me understand more of what it would look like and sound like to give you honor...

I'm also asking the Lord to help me deepen my commitment to His priorities. I first want to love the Lord with all of my heart. After my love for the Lord, I want my priorities to reflect love for my spouse, family, friends, church and the lost – in that order. Could you spend some time telling me how I'm doing with those priorities?

After you've had this conversation with your spouse (or close friend, if unmarried), talk to your pastor/pastor advocate. Make specific plans to address any needed changes.

AN ENCOUNTER WITH JESUS

"And we are confident that he hears us whenever we ask for anything that pleases him. And since we know he hears us when we make our requests, we also know that he will give us what we ask for" (1 John 5:14-15 NLT).

Reflect on the concentric circles above and then pray these humble prayers to the Lord.

God, which of these relationships would You like to see me give more attention? How do You see these relationships and the priorities of my life?

After you've heard from the Lord, pray a prayer that you can be confident He will hear and answer. Pray with confidence because you know these prayers are pleasing to Him.

- God, I ask for You to deepen my love for You. I want to love You more. Help me to experience more of Your love, so I can love you in return.
- God, I ask for You to deepen my love for my spouse. Help me to...
- God, I ask You to strengthen my love for my kids, especially in... God, I ask You to deepen my love for the church, I particularly need You to expand my love for...
- and show me how to...
- God, I ask You to refresh my love for people outside the church. Help me to see people with a renewed sense of...

A MOMENT OF FELLOWSHIP

"Two people are better off than one, for they can help each other succeed" (Ecclesiastes 4:9).

Pray together with your pastor or pastor advocate. Ask God to make any needed changes in the area of priorities. Pray with one another.

Heavenly Father, make any changes in my heart and life that You see are needed. Help me to live out the concentric circle priorities. I specifically ask You to change me by...

Pray for one another.

Heavenly Father, I ask you to help my friend by...

Deepen his love for...

Strengthen the relationship with...

Help me know how to encourage...

AN ENCOUNTER WITH JESUS

"And David became more and more powerful, because the LORD of Heaven's Armies was with him" (1 Chronicles 11:9 NLT).

"Don't be afraid, for I am with you. Don't be discouraged, for I am your God. I will strengthen you and help you. I will hold you up with my victorious right hand" (Isaiah 41:10 NLT).

David was strengthened by the powerful presence of the Lord. David was victorious because the Lord was with him. Reflect for a moment on this truth. The same Lord, who is Lord of Heaven's Armies and was with David, is with you! Jesus doesn't just support men named David who fight battles around Jerusalem, He is with you! Let the prophet Isaiah remind you of God's promise and presence. Soak in the reassuring words of the Lord. Imagine Jesus is sitting beside you and sharing these words:

- Don't be afraid of conflict in the church, I am with you.
- Don't be discouraged of criticism and scrutiny, for I am your God.
- Don't be afraid when attendance isn't what you had hoped, I am with you.
- Don't be discouraged when things take longer than you wanted, I am your God.
- Don't be afraid of change, I am with you.
- Don't be discouraged when family and ministry are hard, for I am your God.
- I will strengthen you. I will help you. I will hold you up with my victorious right hand.

After you have soaked in the promises of the Lord, give Him thanks. Tell Him about your trust and your gratitude.

Lord of Heaven's Armies, I am grateful for your promise to be with me because...

I am grateful for your promise to help me because...

I am trusting You to...

I am counting on You to...and when we are victorious, I will shout your praises because you are my God!

AN EXPERIENCE WITH SCRIPTURE

"Where there is no guidance the people fall,

But in abundance of counselors there is victory" (Proverbs 11:14 NASB).

Make plans to pray with your pastor/pastor advocate. Pray together about who should be invited to be a part of your 30+1 ministry. Pray for the Lord's direction and wisdom. Pray that He would reveal an abundance of counselors.

Lord of Heaven, we want Your guidance as we approach the 30+1 ministry. We know that there is victory in the abundance of counselors, so we're asking you to reveal the best prayer warriors from our church and community. We need trusted, followers of Jesus who will lift up our pastor. Speak, Lord. We are listening. Show us who should be a part of this trusted group of counselors?

A MOMENT OF FELLOWSHIP

"This makes for harmony among the members, so that all the members care for each other" (1 Corinthians 12:25).

Pastors and pastor's advocates: There will be an increase in harmony within your congregation, when members demonstrate care for one another. Creating this kind of caring environment begins with you. Therefore, as the two of you meet together and as you meet with the members of 30+1, make vulnerability and care for one another a priority. Make these conversations a part of your private meetings and then as appropriate, share these responses with the 30+1 group as well.

One of my recent celebrations in life, has been...
One of my recent celebrations in ministry has been...
I have been depending upon God for
I have needed support recently in...
I need your continued prayer for...
I am feeling discouraged about...
I am feeling anxious about...
I am feeling grateful for...
I am praising God for...

AN EXPERIENCE WITH SCRIPTURE

"In my distress I called to the LORD; I cried to my God for help. From his temple he heard my voice; my cry came before him, into his ears" (Psalm 18:6 NIV).

Reflect on your past experiences of "calling out to the Lord," how He heard you and answered your cry. Do you remember times in the past when you found it important to seek the Lord and were glad you did? When have you encountered the challenges of ministry and been blessed because you called upon God? Do you remember crying out to the Lord because you...

- encountered new challenges or obstacles?
- encountered new enemies or attacks?
- faced ministry expansion or redirection?
- were faced with complaints, opposition, or apathy?
- were faced with conflicting demands or priorities?

I remember crying out to the Lord when...

He heard my cry, because...

I am grateful that I went before the Lord because...

Now that you have reaffirmed the benefits of time with the Lord, talk to Him about current needs. Express your faith in how He hears your voice and answers your cry.

AN ENCOUNTER WITH JESUS

Teach us to number our days, that we may gain a heart of wisdom" (Psalm 90:12).

Consider some of the challenges that you face with your relationship with Jesus, your spouse, children, the church or evangelism. How do you struggle with the gift of time He has given you? Share those with Jesus now:

Jesus, I am reminded of how I'm struggling with...

It's difficult for me to know how to...

and I need You to teach me how to...

Give me wisdom in how I spend my time, especially how to...

Express your concerns to Jesus and then allow His Spirit to speak words of care and comfort to your heart. Listen for any changes that the Lord wants for your life.

Imagine Christ is talking to you personally. Listen to His voice as He says,

"I want to share in this challenge with you. I am here for you. Give these cares and burdens to Me. I will teach you how to make the best decisions with your time. I will give you wisdom, because I give generously to those who call on Me. You can count on Me because I love you."

As you finish praying, make plans to talk about this prayer experience with your pastor/pastor advocate. Talk about how much it means to have a God who cares about your life, your challenges and your struggles. Share what the Lord revealed to you and any changes that need to be made in your life.

A MOMENT OF FELLOWSHIP

"Let all that I am praise the LORD; may I never forget the good things he does for me" (Psalm 103:2 NLT).

Close this chapter with a moment of reflection. Allow God to remind you of some of the significant blessings in your life. With all of the pressures of life and ministry, may we never forget the good things that God has done for us. There can be no better use of time than to give praise and honor to the Lord.

Allow God to remind you of a significant blessing in your life.

I remember...

how God recently gave an answer to prayer...

how God met a financial need when ...

how God brought unexplainable peace during a difficult time...

how God brought specific people into my life, just when I needed them...

how God protected me by...

how God guided me and gave me wisdom when...

Pause for a few moments of personal prayer. Tell God about your gratitude. Praise Him for these good things.

God, I am so grateful for the good things that you have brought to my life. I'm especially grateful today for...

I can think of no better way to spend my time than to honor You, so I thank You for...

Finally, share these blessings with your pastor/pastor advocate. Celebrate the goodness of our God together!

APPENDIX 1:

Accountabilty Questions

PERSONAL

1. Have you spent quality and quantity time alone with the Lord each day this week? If the Lord were to bless the Sunday services on the basis of your prayer life this week, what would happen?
   What is the Lord showing you specifically in His Word?
   Have you been up by 6:00am Tuesday, Wednesday, and Thursday at work in your office?
2. Have you shared the Gospel with anyone this week? Tell me about it.
3. Have you looked at anything this week, TV, internet, magazines, etc.…that would be considered inappropriate or questionable?
4. Have you had any conversation with the opposite sex that would be considered inappropriate?
5. Are you at peace with all people as much as it depends upon you?
   Have you gossiped about anyone this week?
   Have you spoken harshly or unkindly to anyone this week?
   Is there any area of disobedience to the Lord in your life?
6. Have you gotten physical exercise this week?

FAMILY

7. Have you spent quality and quality time with (Spouses Name) this week?
   Do you love your wife as Christ loves the church? What have you done specifically to serve her or speak her love language this week?
   Have you had a date-night this month?
8. Have you spent time with (Children's Name) and (Children's Name) this week? Have you encouraged them this week in any way?

9. Have you seen or talked to your mother/father this week? Are you spending time with her at least monthly?

MINISTRY

10. How have you served the staff this week as a leader?
11. Are there any unresolved issues with the staff that you should address?
12. Are you maintaining discipline in your sermon preparation?
13. Are you spending 75% of your time and energy on the 5 Things only you can do?
    - Sermon Prep
    - Leading Staff
    - Giving Vision to Church
    - Spiritually Leading Leaders, Deacons, etc...
    - Ministering to those in major crisis

From Pastor Hank Williams - Boiling Springs Baptist Church

APPENDIX 2:

Sabbatical Information

Dear Friend,

Sabbatical is a wonderful time of refreshment and I'm so glad you are moving toward this being a part of your life. The following packet is an eclectic group of documents, so glean what you wish and toss the rest. Also the sabbatical reports are dated because I now give a verbal report instead of a written one. This is in the form of a 20 minute CD I record and give to our personnel committee to listen to at their convenience. They have liked this approach.

You are wise to prepare well for sabbatical. If you don't time will pass quickly and you will not return having truly been refreshed. Also, I would encourage you to prepare your family well too. Many wives and children assume sabbatical is just a month of Saturdays. "Finally he'll clean the garage out, paint the house, or be my 24/7 playmate." thoughts will clash with your thoughts of "I'm so glad to finally have time to read, rest and strategize. Daddy and hubby "working in a different way" is a good place to start. What works for me is to commit my mornings to Lord and ministry preparation and my afternoons to family. The evenings are a toss-up depending on the night. I'm not legalistic about this morning/evening schedule; it just helps to set expectations and rhythm. I want to forgo the sad family faces as I get the day started by them knowing they will get me at lunch. My days move from 30 minute appointments to morning, afternoon and night. Ahh, feels good to just type it (before I race to my 11:30 lunch meeting).

Lastly, though you may not want to, it is important that you communicate well how your sabbatical was used and what difference it made for your ministry. The typical church member will think you have just been on a "spiritualize vacation" people in the "real world" don't get. So your communication should help teach them and also build trust in you that the time was well spent. Don't let this produce bitterness or guilt in you, but wisdom of the best way to spend your time and the best way to communicate it to those who approved and paid for it. By doing this through the years, I have seen our church move from scratching their heads wondering about it, to celebrating my time away. Also the trust that I have built with the church in my communication has resulted in our sabbatical policy extending to other ministers besides the pastor (every 7 years for the four men that report to me and every 10 years for other ministers). Trust is the currency of ministry. Trust in the Lord by you and the trust of the people in you. Clear communication builds trust.

I hope this packet helps you to have a wonderful sabbatical. The Lord wants you refreshed and the saw sharpened. Now is the time to focus on both.

Gregg Matte

In Jesus,
Gregg Matte

Included:

- Sabbatical thoughts
- HFBC Sabbatical Policy for Category Level 1 ministers & Category Level 2a ministers

713.681.8000 . HoustonsFirst.org . 7401 katy freeway . houston tx 77024

APPENDIX 3:

Pastor and Advocate Convenant

PASTOR ADVOCATE COVENANT

PRACTICAL COMMITMENTS AND COVENANT

a. Willingness to serve alongside and support the pastor
b. Keep all conversations confidential
c. Support the Pastor "no matter what"
d. Guard my Pastor's time
e. Speak honestly to my Pastor
f. Faithfully attend the church services
g. Proclaim the gospel to unbelievers
h. Be actively involved in discipleship
i. Faithfully tithe

I commit to faithfully advocate for my Pastor.

ADVOCATE SIGNATURE DATE

PASTOR SIGNATURE DATE

Covenant to be reviewed yearly and re-committed to by both parties

Download this covenant at: ***www.liftyourpastor.com***

APPENDIX 4:

How to Find an Advocate

Pray specifically for God to lead you to an advocate – another man who has a sincere walk with the Lord and an encouraging heart toward you.

Ask your spouse about potential advocates – many times our spouse has an intuition of who would be an encourager and support to you.

Once you have identified a potential advocate, pray over that name for a few weeks.

Ask your spouse again about this potential advocate, have them to join you in prayer.

Have a meeting with potential advocate sharing your heart for friendship and mutual support. Give them a copy of Lift Your Pastor book.

Invite the potential advocate to read the Lift Your Pastor book over the next month and pray about joining you as an advocate.

If the answer is yes, meet once every 4 to 6 weeks and journey together through the Lift Your Pastor book. Spend time in your meeting going through the Experiencing Scripture, Encountering Jesus & Engaging in fellowship sections of the book.

Complete a "Relational Needs Survey" at:
www.greatcommandment.net and discover and share with each other your top 3 relational needs.

If there begin to be any struggles or concerns with the pastor/advocate relationship, go back to specific chapters and discuss again.

Consider attending a Pastor/Advocate conference together.
(more details at **www.liftyourpastor.com**)

ABOUT THE AUTHORS

DR. MICHAEL LEWIS

SENIOR PASTOR

Roswell Street Baptist Church, Marietta , GA

Since April, 2016 Dr. Lewis has had the privilege of serving as the lead pastor at Roswell Street Baptist Church in Marietta, Georgia.

Dr. Michael Lewis is a pastor who desires to lead individuals to follow Jesus on a mission to love God, love people, and lead others to do the same.

He is a graduate of Columbia International University, Southeastern Baptist Theological Seminary. He was awarded an honorary doctorate from Liberty University in 2005. He has pastored churches in Florida, South Carolina, and Texas. He served 3 years with the North American Mission Board as the 'pastor to pastors' around the United States and overseas.

Dr. Lewis grew up in Savannah. He has been serving as a pastor since he was 21 years old.

He has been married to Liliana. She is a native of Mexico City. They have three daughters.

ANDREW MCKINLEY SPENCER

Andrew McKinley Spencer was born in Corpus Christi, Texas in 1968. Andy attended Mary Carroll High School. Andy received his Eagle Scout award in 1978 at Troop 11 sponsored by First Baptist Church.

Mr. Spencer received a BBA in Entrepreneurship/Marketing from Baylor University.. While at Baylor, Andy served as the Baylor Mascot and received the Best Mascot Award at NCA Camp in 1986.

Andy joined the Arthur Valve and Fitting Company in 1987 as a salesperson in San Antonio, Texas. Andy served in various sales, management and executive roles in his 15 years with the company. In January of 2002, Andy purchased the company and renamed it Arthur Fluid System Technologies.

On February 1, 2010, Andy sold Arthur Fluid System Technologies. Andy now runs a consulting business as well as commercial real estate investments.

In 2012, Andy formed Take 5 Ministries, an organization providing leadership development for Pastors through peer-to-peer learning experiences.

Andy has published a book *"Leadership from the Sidelines – Much of What I Learned about Leadership, I Learned as a Mascot."* and has formed a publishing company helping Pastors publish their books.

Andy is continually educating himself and others in areas ranging from basic selling skills to efficiency training, change management and team building. Andy has spoken to classes at Baylor University, Emanuel Baptist University in Romania, Seminary Bonn in Germany as well as industry conferences.

Andy serves as a Deacon at Great Hills Baptist Church in Austin, Texas. Andy has also served in Church leadership as Personnel Committee Chairman and Chairman of the Deacons.

Andy's family includes his wife Kathy and two daughters Deanna and Andrea. They live in northwest Austin and are active in church and community activities.

ACKNOWLEDGEMENTS

[A] *Dr David Ferguson – Great Commandment Network*

[B] *North American Mission Board Pastoral Care*

For more information on receiving additional copies (print or PDF) of Lift Your Pastor – Becoming a Pastor's Advocate, go to ***www.liftyourpastor.com*** *and click on "**Book**"*

Made in the USA
San Bernardino, CA
27 July 2018